HARVARD SLAVIC STUDIES
V

HARVARD
SLAVIC STUDIES

EDITORIAL COMMITTEE

Managing Editor

HORACE G. LUNT

Associate Editors

ALBERT B. LORD   WIKTOR WEINTRAUB

VSEVOLOD SETCHKAREV   ROBERT A. ROTHSTEIN

VOLUME V

HARVARD UNIVERSITY PRESS

Cambridge, Massachusetts

1 9 7 0

© Copyright 1970 by the President and Fellows of Harvard College

All rights reserved

Distributed in Great Britain by Oxford University Press, London

Library of Congress Catalog Card Number: 52–12516

SBN 674–37804–0

Printed in Great Britain

CONTENTS

HARVARD SLAVIC STUDIES

V

THE ORIGINS OF THE
WAR FOR A SERBIAN LANGUAGE
AND ORTHOGRAPHY

Thomas Butler

During the first half of the nineteenth century, Serbian intellectuals were involved in an intense debate about the kind of literary language their emerging nation should adopt. The controversy became so fierce that one contestant, Ðura Daničić, called it the "war for a Serbian language and orthography."

Serbs had never developed a significant secular literature, and in their religious books and chronicles had employed the traditional Church Slavonic language. In the seventeenth century the local variant, which may be called Serbian Slavonic, became gradually modified under the influence of the Russian Slavonic, which had been established in the Russian Empire by the Nikonian reforms. Lacking their own printing presses, the Serbs imported books from Russia in increasing numbers, so that by the early years of the eighteenth century, Russian Slavonic had been accepted for all purposes by the Orthodox theocracy. Subsequently the reviving Serbian national spirit, nourished by the enlightened educational program for national minorities instituted by the Austrian Emperor Joseph II, inspired some intellectuals to attack the hegemony of this archaic language. The leader of the Serbian movement was a renegade monk, Dositej Obradović (1742–1811), who believed that the use of Russian Slavonic had prevented the growth of literacy among his people. He proposed that Serbs simplify the Slavonic alphabet of forty-two letters and write in a language close to the vernacular.

Writers began to use the spoken language in their works. The experienced novelist Milovan Vidaković, in the introduction to Part I of his *Ljubomir u Elisiumu* (Ljubomir in Elisium) published in 1814,

1

promised that henceforth he would write in a language "above the kitchen" but so close to the common speech that everyone would understand it. Vidaković and other writers expected, however, that the new literary idiom would incorporate elements of Russian Slavonic, which they regarded as a perfected language. But because the language movement was disorganized and there was no agreement on which features of Russian Slavonic to retain, each writer worked out his own particular mixture, which was loosely known as Slaveno-Serbian. To establish a norm, Vidaković called for a language congress and the writing of a Serbian grammar.

In 1814 in Vienna, Vuk Karadžić (1787–1864) added his voice to the growing national discussion. In the Foreword to his *Pismenica* (short grammar) Karadžić proposed that Serbian writers adhere completely to the peasant speech and that they eliminate all Russian Slavonic elements from their writing. He later (1815) published an insulting critique of an early Vidaković novel, claiming that the novelist did not know Serbian. This attack began the Serbian linguistic controversy, which was to last for half a century. In the end the Karadžić forces won, and they and their spiritual descendants have set the course of Serbian philology down to the present time. It is not surprising, therefore, that Vuk's figure towers above all others in Serbian articles and books about the language movement. His opponents, the Slaveno-Serbs, are usually depicted as narrow-minded, ignorant, or misguided, under the control of a reactionary church. No consideration is given to the fact that the Slaveno-Serbian proposals had a strong practical justification.

The Vuk-centered frame of reference traditionally used in discussing the Serbian language controversy is much too confining for an objective account. This study rather begins with Vuk's mentor, Jernej Kopitar, and relates Kopitar's theories to the views of other linguists of his day. Nor is it meaningful to speak of the Slaveno-Serbs without reference to the history of earlier Serbian writing. In the absence of any straightforward treatment of the written language prior to Vuk's reforms, the earlier period is discussed extensively here. The major focus, however, is on the debate between Milovan Vidaković and Vuk Karadžić, for a close examination of their disagreement illuminates the deeply emotional as well as intellectual issues that exacerbated the struggle.

I. JERNEJ KOPITAR

Jernej Kopitar was born August 21, 1780, in the village of Repnje, Carniola Province, Slovenia. Slovenia was then a part of the Hapsburg Empire, as it had been for centuries. In his autobiography Kopitar reported that his father was a "polovicar" or "possessor of half a hide of land."[1] Kopitar's peasant origins were obvious when he started school in Ljubljana, for he knew "not a syllable of German," at a time when mainly German was spoken in Slovene towns, or, among the lower classes, a mixture of German and Slovene. In the schools of his province the Carniolan dialect was used only in the first year; it was then supplanted by German, and by the fourth year the language of instruction was Latin. Greek was an obligatory subject in the gymnasium.[2]

Young Kopitar showed unusual linguistic talent, which was a great advantage in the educational system established by the Austrian Emperor Joseph II (1741–1790). At the end of the third grade the peasant boy from Repnje received a prize for being the best student in his class of 250 boys. In subsequent years, in recognition of his superior academic standing, Kopitar received free tuition plus a stipend of fifty guilders. After his parents died during a plague in 1794, he managed to continue his education, living off his stipend as well as fees for tutoring weaker students. In 1799, at the end of his formal studies, Kopitar became tutor to the nephew of Baron Sigismund Zois, and later he entered Zois's service as secretary, librarian, and curator of his mineral cabinets. In the Baron's library Kopitar continued his study of classical Greek and Latin, as well as the modern European languages. He read the works of Dante, Boccaccio, Petrarch, Machiavelli, Ariosto, Tasso, and Metastasio, besides learning to read English "from the six beautiful volumes of Gibbon."

Baron Zois had accumulated a remarkably complete library of Slavic printed materials and manuscripts, particularly in the South

---

1. Jernej Kopitar, "Selbstbiographie," in *Kleinere Schriften*, I (cited hereafter as *KS*). For full information on all works cited in notes, see Bibliography. Note that the German form of Kopitar's given name, Bartholomäus, appears on his writings; Jernej is the Slovene equivalent.
2. Nestor M. Petrovskij, *Pervye gody dejatel'nosti V. Kopitarja*, pp. 7–8.

Slavic languages.[3] His library contained almost everything Slavic that had been printed in Venice and elsewhere in Italy. No mere dilettante, the Baron studied these documents and had a reasonably clear idea of the features distinguishing Slovene from the other Slavic languages. When the Freising Fragments were discovered, Zois identified them as Slovene. He wished to see Slovene reestablished as a literary language, and as a first step toward developing a normalized literary language, he sought the creation of "philosophical-critical" grammars and dictionaries. Zois attracted to this project a group of scholars, including Jurij Japelj, Blaž Kumerdej, Anton Linhart, and Valentin Vodnik, all of whom were equally dedicated to the rehabilitation of the Slovene language. Indeed, it was through Zois's influence that Vodnik, a Catholic monk and a well-known poet, was transferred to Ljubljana so that he could take part in the lexicographical work. Vodnik spent the rest of his life writing a German-Slovene dictionary, which was never finished. Zois and his brother contributed to the dictionary project a special supplement of several hundred terms from the fields of botany, zoology, and mineralogy. They gleaned these words from among the country folk, because they knew that the townspeople were not valid informants for pure Slovene.

In 1806, during the occupation of Slovenia by a Napoleonic army, Baron Zois was asked by the daughter of the French commandant in Ljubljana to find her a Slovene tutor, "because the best cooks in Ljubljana speak only Carniolan." Kopitar readily agreed to teach the pretty young French girl enough Slovene to manage her household. More than thirty years later, in his autobiography, the veteran scholar recalled that happy time with his bright and attractive pupil, but he referred disparagingly to his Slovene *Grammatik* (Grammar)[4] which, he claimed, was the direct outgrowth of the five or six pages of tables he had written for the young Countess. Subsequent bio-

---

3. The Zois contribution to early Slavic studies seems to have been considerable, but unfortunately there is little factual information about him. The sources used here are Kopitar, "Selbstbiographie"; Petrovskij, *Pervye gody*; France Kidrič, *Dobrovský in Slovenski preporod njegove dobe*; *Korespondenca Sigmunda Barona Zoisa 1808–1809*; and the biography of Kopitar in the *Slovenski biografski leksikon*.

4. Kopitar, *Grammatik der slavischen Sprache in Krain, Kärnten und Steyermark*.

graphers, including Nestor Petrovskij, have accepted Kopitar's excuse for the inadequacies of his first work, failing to appreciate the absurdity of associating the massively documented, 460-page *Grammatik* with his minor tutorial materials. The *Grammatik* was actually the fruit of Kopitar's years with Zois, and it may well have been the underlying reason for his employment. The brilliant young gymnasium graduate may have been hired in the hope that one day he would write the "philosophical-critical" grammar needed to provide the basis for new practical grammars of the Slovene literary language. His later depreciation of the work notwithstanding, Kopitar's *Grammatik* accomplished this purpose.[5]

In 1808 Kopitar went to Vienna where, after studying law for about two years, he decided to enter the Austrian Imperial Library as a "scriptor." He finally obtained the position through the help of the Czech "Patriarch of Slavistics," Josef Dobrovský, with whom he had begun a correspondence in 1808. Kopitar was obsessed with the thought that Austria was really a Slavic state, and in an early letter to Dobrovský he complained, "In the library of an Emperor whose state is three-quarters composed of Slavs, they pay no attention to Slavica."[6] Indeed, in his letter of application to the Emperor, Kopitar stressed that Vienna, not St. Petersburg, was the true center of the Slavic world, for "short radii" emanated from it to all the Slavic tribes.[7] One of the Slovene's early duties in the library was to censor the Slavic, Rumanian, Greek, and Albanian books produced within the Empire.

At the beginning of the nineteenth century Vienna was the most important gathering place for South Slav intellectuals; it was also a center for the German Romantic movement.[8] Competition between German and Slavic national aspirations abated during the Napoleonic Wars, when Slavs were especially popular with Germans because of the Russian resistance to Napoleon. The three "Russian

---

5. Discussions of the influence of Kopitar's work may be found in Petrovskij, *Pervye gody*, pp. 220–236; Robert Auty, "The Formation of the Slovene Literary Language."

6. Joseph Dobrovský, *Briefwechsel zwischen Dobrowský und Kopitar (1808–1828)*, p. 51 (cited hereafter as *BDK*).

7. *Kopitarjeva spomenica*, p. 126.

8. See *Kopitars Briefwechsel mit Karl Georg Rumy*, p. 7; Mathias Murko, *Die deutsche Einflüsse*, p. 1.

quartets" of Beethoven (the seventh, eighth, and ninth) were commissioned in 1806 by the Russian ambassador to Vienna, Count Andrej Razumovskij.[9] Kopitar contributed to Friedrich Schlegel's *Deutsches Museum*, a journal published in Vienna in 1812–1813, and their collaboration as editors on the *Wiener allgemeine Literaturzeitung*, published in 1813–1816, is further evidence of the coexistence of the German and Slavic idea in Vienna during this period.

Schlegel's theories on national literature and language, summarized in his 1812 Vienna lectures on "The History of Ancient and Modern Literature" and later published as *Geschichte der Alten und Neuen Literatur*, were readily adopted by the South Slavs as basic premises for their own cultural rebirth. South Slavs such as Kopitar, whose Slovene countrymen were still writing in German, Italian, or Latin, or his Serbian friends, the medical students Dimitrije Davidović and Dimitrije Frušić, whose countrymen were writing in German, Hungarian,[10] Russian Slavonic, or the new Slaveno-Serbian mixtures, could hardly fail to see the parallel between their own present-day situation and the recent German experience described by Schlegel:

> Our men of letters until recently were completely cut off from the rest of society, and fully separated from . . . the upper class, just as they were from the rest of the people. Our Kepler and Leibnitz wrote mainly in Latin; Frederick the Great read, wrote, and thought only in French. The mother tongue was badly neglected both by the scholars and the aristocracy. National memories and feelings were left . . . to the common people, who still retained some, albeit weak and half-garbled, relics of the good old times.

Schlegel's generalizations about the rights of nations to their own language and literature were like war cries to the Slavic intellectuals:[11]

---

9. L. S. Sinjaver, *Žizn' Betxovena*, pp. 147–149.

10. Lukijan Mušickij addressed his "Oda mojemu prijatelju Mihailu Vitkoviću" to a Serb who preferred to write in Hungarian (1811). Kopitar commented on this poem in *Wiener allgemeine Literaturzeitung* two years later; see *KS*, pp. 209–210.

11. Murko, *Die deutsche Einflüsse*, pp. 4–5, points out that Schlegel's views "gradually became flesh and blood for the Austrian Slavs."

A nation which allows herself to be deprived of her language loses her last hold on her inner, spiritual independence, and actually ceases to exist . . .
Every important and independent nation has . . . the right to possess its own . . . literature, and the worst barbarism is that which oppresses the language of a people and a land, or which would exclude it from all higher intellectual activity. Also, it is only a prejudice if one regards languages which have been neglected or, very frequently, which are unknown to us, as being incapable of a higher perfection.

Schlegel maintained that some nationalities, lacking a significant written literature, might possess the finest cultural heritage of all:

National recollections, the noblest inheritance a people can possess, are an advantage which nothing else can replace; for when a people are exalted in their feelings and ennobled by the consciousness that they have had a great past, that such recollections have come down to them from the oldest times—in a word, that they have a national poetry of their own, then they should be ranked at a high level.[12]

Another famous German scholar whom Kopitar came to know in 1812 was the outstanding philosopher-linguist Wilhelm von Humboldt, then Prussian Ambassador to Vienna. In June 1812, in a letter to Dobrovský, Kopitar mentioned that he had met "Vater's rival in language study" and that the Ambassador had decided to study "Slavic" with him after finishing his study of Hungarian. From other letters to Dobrovský it is clear that Humboldt studied Czech with Kopitar, using Dobrovský's *Geschichte der böhmischen Sprache und ältern Literatur* (History of the Czech Language and Older Literature), *Ausführliches Lehrgebäude der böhmischen Sprache* (Detailed System of the Czech Language), and the journal *Slavin*. Kopitar considered these to be "the most philosophically elaborated among all the Slavic [works]." In that same year, while scholars in Prague, Vienna, and Ljubljana were participating in a Dobrovský-led debate concerning the identity of the Freising Fragments, Humboldt requested that the Fragments be sent to him from Munich so that he and Kopitar could

---

12. Schlegel, *Geschichte der alten und neuen Literatur*, pp. 9, 218, 229, 15–16. All translations are my own.

examine them, and some sample copper plates could be made for publication.[13]

Humboldt devoted many years to the study of the Basque language. In December 1812, in the *Deutsches Museum*, he published a long article entitled, "Ankündigung einer Schrift über die vaskische Sprache und Nation, nebst Angabe des Gesichtspunktes und Inhalts derselben," (Announcement of a Work on the Basque Language and Nation, with a Sketch of the Viewpoint and the Contents of the Same). He speculated about the influence of race and environment on the development of man's "original tendencies"—a theory that Kopitar cited with alacrity in an article he wrote shortly afterward, giving an etymologically based "proof" of the Slavic origin of Lessing (*Les-ing) and Leibnitz (*Lip-niza): "If it is therefore true, as Humboldt in his profound announcement of his work on the Basque language maintains, that the 'race contributes significantly to the original tendencies,' how perfectible must the Slavic race be, to which a Leibnitz and a Lessing originally belonged."[14]

Humboldt opposed the writing of grammars based on Latin categories. He felt that each language possesses its own system, which has developed so as to reflect a people's own experience with its environment. For him no language has gaps or inadequacies. A recent German writer claims: "Humboldt is in opposition to the whole of linguistic science of the nineteenth century, in that he is not historically-oriented, but urges synchronically oriented linguistics."[15] In fact, Kopitar shared this synchronic approach, in the areas of both grammar writing and orthographical systematization. The coincidence is not remarkable when one considers that both men were influenced by the writings of the Berlin academician, Johann Christoph Adelung.

Adelung published his *Deutsche Sprachlehre zum Gebrauche der Schulen in den König. Preuss. Länden* (German Grammar for the Use of Schools in the Royal Prussian Lands) in Berlin in 1781, and his *Umständliches Lehrgebäude der deutschen Sprache zur Erläuterung*

13. Dobrovský, *BDK*, pp. 272, 288, 297.

14. Kopitar, "Leibnitz und Lessing," *Wiener allgemeine Literaturzeitung*, 1813, reprinted in *KS*, p. 163.

15. Brigit Beneš, *Wilhelm von Humboldt, Jacob Grimm, August Schleicher*, p. 4.

der deutschen Sprachlehre für Schulen (Detailed System of the German Language for the Explanation of German Grammar for Schools) in Leipzig in 1782, not long after Kopitar was born. These books later provided the Slovene's basic linguistic platform. Adelung opposed the use of Latin categories in the new grammars, and in principle he favored a synchronic treatment:

> Almost all the grammars of the new languages, and thus not German alone, have formed most of their rules according to the Latin grammars; therefore they are as a whole so faulty and so incomplete that they are inadequate for a thorough mastery of a language ... As a language rises and falls with the knowledge and culture of a people, so too must the language rules be adapted in a most precise manner to the actual circumstances of a language. They must not set the language back half or whole centuries, and even less should they anticipate centuries, since no mortal can know what the future holds for a whole culture and, consequently, for a language too... [The grammarian] is not the lawgiver of a people, but only the collector and the publisher of the laws made by them, their spokesman and the interpreter of their intentions. He never decides but only collects the votes cast by the majority ... He presents the language as it really is, not as it could be, or as it should be in his imagination.

With orthography, Adelung again is synchronic *in principle*, but he is realistic enough to foresee that the *interpreter* in the linguist will occasionally have to give the *collector* some assistance:

> The script should make visible to the eyes the audible sounds, in so far as they are symbols of thoughts and images: therefore, it follows that it can and should express no other sounds than those heard in the utterance, and nothing else except what is really heard. Therefore, the first basic law for the writing of all languages is: *write as you speak* ...
> One writes therefore each clearly heard, simple sound with its own symbol, but writes also nothing more than what is actually heard in pronunciation ...
> Write German and what is considered as German with the established letters, just as you speak, in conformity with the best general pronunciation, with consideration of the closest proved derivation, and, where this is not helpful, of common usage.[16]

16. Johann C. Adelung, *Umständliches Lehrgebäude der deutschen Sprache zur Erläuterung der deutschen Sprachlehre für Schulen*, pp. 112–114; *Deutsche Sprachlehre zum Gebrauche der Schulen in den König. Preuss. Länden*, pp. 577, 580; *Vollständiger Anweisung zur deutschen Orthographie*, p. 117.

While still in Ljubljana, Kopitar had become familiar with Adelung's theories. The German's linguistic writings were known to other members of the Zois group, including Vodnik, who used Adelung's *Grammatisch-kritisches Wörterbuch der hochdeutschen Mundart* (Grammatical-Critical Dictionary of the High German Dialect 1793–1801), as the basis for his Slovene dictionary. Vodnik sent Dobrovský a letter concerning this project, to which the Czech Slavicist replied on March 3, 1808, with an outline of Adelung's theories.[17] A year later Kopitar, in the *Grammatik* (p. 152), quoted the *Umständliches Lehrgebäude der deutschen Sprache* to support his criticism of Bohorič's Slovene orthography. Zois's librarian had good reason to appreciate the wisdom of the Prussian's dictum, "Write as you speak," for in his books and manuscripts he could see the orthographical anarchy then prevailing in the Slavic lands. In the *Grammatik* (p. xxvi) he castigated six different users of Latin letters for their variances: "The Slavs in Carniola have one [orthography], in Dalmatia another, in Croatia a third, in Bohemia a fourth, in Poland a fifth, and in Lausitz a sixth." Moreover, there was no internal uniformity within some groups: "In Dalmatia, for example, a Dellabella writes in one way, a Voltiggi in another, and still another person in another way." Kopitar gave a table showing the different spellings for certain words among the six Latin-users; for example: *fhzhuka, sctuka, schuka, štika, szczuka,* and *fczuka.* He echoed August von Schlözer, on whose historical data he relied, about the necessity for a uniform alphabet and orthography for "the Latin half" of Slavdom.[18] According to Kopitar, contemporary differences in orthography were attractive only to "Slavic dilletantes." It is difficult to decide whether lack of travel outside Slovenia, Pan-Slavic idealism, or a combination of the two led Kopitar to overlook major differences among the Slavic languages. He ignored the fact that orthographical discrepancies often reflected basic phonemic distinctions, or that the current dogma regarding "Slavic" as one great language with several dialects was obsolete.

When Kopitar became censor for Slavic, Rumanian, Greek, and Albanian books, he perceived the woeful lack of agreement on

17. Petrovskij, *Pervye gody*, p. 39.
18. August von Schlözer wrote the influential *Allgemeine nordische Geschichte* and *Nestor*, both of which Kopitar quoted in the *Grammatik*.

orthography among the writers of the newly evolving national litera-
tures. His articles during his first years in Vienna reflected continuing
concern with the need for standardization. Nor did he confine his
attention to the Slavic peoples. He followed closely the efforts of
Adamantios Korais (1748–1833) to fuse elements of ancient and
modern Greek into a new Greek literary language, and he studied
Rumanian attempts at language reform. One of the best statements
of Kopitar's principles may be found in his long review in 1813 of
Peter Major's *Geschichte des Ursprungs der Römer in Dacien* (History
of the Origin of the Romans in Dacia).[19] Frequently derisive,
Kopitar discussed Major's proposal that Rumanians, as true heirs
of Rome, should base the alphabet of their new literary language on
the Latin. The Slovene classicist reminded the author that the Latin
alphabet had been inadequate for the Latin language itself during
different historical periods. For the Rumanians, he advocated retention of the modified Cyrillic alphabet that they had hitherto been
using: "Because the Romans wrote with Latin letters, these half-
Romans, in blind bias, also wish to use no other than the Latin,
without considering that the Cyrillic alphabet has as many simple
letters as their half-Latin language now has sounds, namely 27"
(*KS*, 240). Kopitar believed that the main function of an alphabet
was "facilitation of communication." But in spite of his own
rationalism he was forced, in view of the burgeoning Romantic
movement, to recognize that the new alphabet-makers felt themselves patriotically obliged to retain the symbols of a partly real,
partly fictional national past. In such situations he insisted that they
retain only those elements of past writing systems that had a function
in the present phonemic system: "Take from it, in God's name,
those symbols which correspond to the sounds in your language"
(*KS*, 241).

Kopitar opposed the modification of Latin letters for sounds that
did not have a corresponding symbol in the Latin alphabet. He
advised the Rumanians, and elsewhere the Croats and Slovenes, not
to attempt to adapt Latin letters. He criticized the Poles for using
"Teutonic combinations" and the Czechs for their "fly specks," as
he called diacritical marks. Instead, he favored the invention of new

19. Reviewed in *Literaturzeitung*, reprinted in *KS*, pp. 230–243.

letters for peculiarly Slavic or Rumanian sounds. Kopitar stated this position as early as the *Grammatik* (p. 202), when he remarked that twenty Latin letters could be directly adopted by a new alphabet for the Latin half of the Slavic world. He expressed hope that a "Second Cyril" would invent "new, analogical letters" for the remaining sounds. For this role he chose Josef Dobrovský. Kopitar believed that once the Latin Slavs had a common alphabet, they need only to follow Adelung's dictum, and "dialect" differences would disappear in time. Elsewhere he spoke of the need for a universal Slavic alphabet, and he dreamed of the day when all Slavs would be writing in the same literary language. Kopitar frequently cited the ancient Greek tribes who, he claimed, once used a common alphabet but wrote in their individual dialects until a single literary language had evolved (*Grammatik*, 204).

While serving as Zois's librarian, Kopitar had become aware of the anarchy in Serbian writing. He realized that there was no normalized literary language and orthography, and that learned men often wrote in an idiom that was incomprehensible to the uneducated. After he moved to Vienna, Kopitar began to study Serbian. His Serbian friends told him about the efforts of some of their countrymen, including Dositej Obradović, to write in a language that was close to the vernacular and understandable to all. Because there was no grammar and dictionary of the spoken language, Kopitar made a chart of the differences between Serbian and Slovene, basing it partly on the language of Obradović and Emanuilo Janković.[20] He quickly mastered Serbian, and in 1811 he published a nearly faultless translation of part of Pavle Solarić's *Graždansko Zemljeopisanie* (Geography in Civil Letters).[21] Kopitar also wrote several articles bringing the works of Obradović to the attention of European scholars.[22] He quickly grasped the Serb's importance to his nation:

20. Ljubomir Stojanović, *Život i rad Vuka Stef. Karadžića*, p. 21.

21. Pavle Solarić's work was published in Venice in 1804. Kopitar published a long excerpt from it: "A Geography of Bessarabia, Moldavia, Wallachia, Bulgaria, Bosnia, Mount Athos, and Montenegro. From the Serbian," *KS*, pp. 76–79.

22. Kopitar translated and published "Bruchstücke" from Obradović's autobiography, *Život i priključenija*, including the "Letter to Haralampije," as well as a "Vollständiger Auszug" from the same work and a eulogy to the "Serbian Anacharsis." All three are reprinted in *KS*, pp. 49–56, 79–94, and 113–120.

"Among the Illyrians (Serbs) he is the first who in his writing replaced the dead old Slavonic literary language by the living dialect of the people" (*KS*, 119–120). Kopitar echoed Obradović's demand for a simplified alphabet for secular writing.

By far the most significant evidence of Kopitar's early knowledge of the Serbian language situation was his review of *Novine Serbske*.[23] The only Serbian newspaper of the time, the *News* first appeared in August 1813. Kopitar's review, issued several months later in the *Wiener allgemeine Literaturzeitung*, criticized the Serbian paper for both Germanisms and Slavonisms. He particularly disliked the use of the letter ы, which stood for a sound nonexistent in Serbian, and the "space-gobbling" and totally superfluous ъ. He recommended to editors Frušić and Davidović that they read Sava Mrkalj's pamphlet on the Serbian alphabet, *Salo debeloga jera, libo Azbukoprotres* (Fat of the Thick Jer, Or An Alphabet Analysis).[24] This essay had been severely criticized by the Serbian Orthodox hierarchy because Mrkalj proposed to simplify the traditional Slavonic alphabet for secular use, by eliminating letters that were duplicates or stood for sounds not in the Serbian language. The clergy had charged that dropping letters such as ы would cause the modern orthography to come into "collision" with the Slavonic. Kopitar's review defended Mrkalj, citing Russian spellings that correspond to Russian speech and not Slavonic. He suggested, as Dositej Obradović had done earlier, that Serbs keep the orthography of the church language separate from that of the living language they would use in their new literature.

Kopitar minimized dialect differences among the Serbs and Croats, just as in his *Grammatik* he had ignored major differences among the Slavic languages. In an article on Joachim Stulli's *Lexicon latino-italico-illyricum* (Latin-Italian-Illyrian Dictionary), Kopitar

23. Kopitar, "Serbische Literatur," *KS*, pp. 257–265. My colleague Berislav Nikolić of the Belgrade "Institute for the Serbo-Croatian Language" has informed me that among Vuk's papers was found a handwritten review of *Novine Serbske* similar to Kopitar's, "but different nonetheless. The date February, 1814, is written on it, perhaps in Kopitar's hand." Not having had the opportunity to compare the two reviews, I am unable to comment on the relationship between them.

24. Published in Buda, 1810. Reprinted in Karadžić, *Skupljeni gramatički i polemički spisi*, I, 209–218 (cited hereafter as *SG*).

stated: "The Slavic language in Istria, Military Croatia, Dalmatia, Bosnia, and Serbia (including the Serbs who settled in Slavonia and Hungary), except for some provincialisms, is the same."[25] This gross simplification may have been decisive in determining the character of the future Serbo-Croatian literary language.

II. VUK AND KOPITAR: THE FIRST MONTHS IN VIENNA

In his review of *Novine Serbske* Kopitar wrote that the Serbs were still waiting for a "Hercules-Korais" to clean out the "Augean stable" of their literary language, just as Korais was doing for the Greeks. It is likely that when his article was published in April 1814, Kopitar already suspected who the Serbian "Hercules" was to be, having several months earlier met Vuk Stefanović Karadžić. A native of Turkish-controlled Serbia, Vuk had filled minor posts in the Karađorđe revolutionary government, and when it was suppressed he had fled to Vienna, to escape the Turkish revenge and improve his education. Here is his own description of his first meeting with Kopitar:

> I came to Vienna somewhere around midfall 1813, and after writing a small booklet there (as a letter to Karađorđe Petrović), I went to have it printed at the end of that year. This manuscript of mine came into the hands of Mr. Kopitar, as censor, and when he recognized from it . . . that I was a man of the people, and that I was different from all the Serbs he had seen and known up to then, he came to my place to see me. And having got acquainted with me in this way, he persuaded me little by little not only to write down the *folk songs*, but also the *words* [dictionary] and the *Grammar* (*SG*, III, 66).

No copies of the "Letter to Karađorđe Petrović" have survived, and whether it was ever published is not known. But within some months of this meeting Vuk had written down the first book of folk songs or *Pjesnarica*, compiled a short grammar or *Pismenica*, and prepared a critique of *Usamljeni Junoša* (The Lone Youth), a novel by Milovan Vidaković, the most popular Serbian writer of the day.[26]

25. Kopitar, "Joachim Stulli," *Annalen der Literatur und Kunst, Jahrg. 1809* In *KS*, p. 14.

26. *Mala prostonarodnja slaveno-serbska pěsnarica; Pismenica serbskoga jezika po govoru prostoga naroda napisana Vukom Stefanovićem Serbijancem;* "Recenzia (poslana učrednikom nov. serb. na upotreblenie) o knizi zovomoj: Usamlenyj junoša, in *SG*, I, 81–86.

Kopitar asked Karadžić to prepare the *Pjesnarica* first, because of the lofty position assigned to oral literature in the new cultural achievement scale being advanced by the Romantics. Goethe's translation of the "Hasanaginica" ("Was ist Weisses dort am grünen Walde? Ist es Schnee wohl, oder sind es Schwäne?")[27] had led Europeans to conjecture about the possible existence of other such Slavic folksongs. Kopitar had referred to the Goethe translation in his *Grammatik* (p. 176), and after moving to Vienna, he learned from Serbian students that songs like the "Hasanaginica" were still being sung in parts of their homeland. When the Croatian Bishop Maximilian Vrhovac visited Vienna in 1810, Kopitar persuaded him to ask his parish priests to write down the local songs, but evidently this approach to collecting was unsuccessful.[28] Now in 1814, through the efforts of Vuk, Europe was given the evidence that a rich store of songs still flourished among the South Slavs. The *Pjesnarica* attracted the attention of Europe's foremost scholar of oral literature, Jakob Grimm, who began to learn Serbian and ultimately reviewed the book for the *Wiener allgemeine Literaturzeitung* in September 1815.[29]

Vuk's other two works at this time, the *Pismenica* and the critique of *Usamljeni Junoša*, were generated by Kopitar's interest in the creation of a purely Serbian literary language. Karadžić had referred briefly to the language situation in the Foreword to his *Pjesnarica*. He justified the simplified orthography in that book by pointing out that no accepted Serbian standards existed: "I could not decide whom to follow, because not only do no two people approve of one another and write in the same way, but no one writes the same way himself consistently, but today it is this way and tomorrow that way." Vuk called for agreement by learned Serbs on a grammar and dictionary, so that everyone would write according to the same rules and orthography. The *Pjesnarica*'s orthography showed Kopitar's influence and a purposeful negation of the kind of Slaveno-Serbian

27. Goethe's "Klaggesang von der edlen Frauen des Asan Aga" was published by Johann Herder in Vol. I of his *Volkslieder* (1778). Goethe based his version on the German and Serbian texts given by Werthes in a translation of Alberto Fortis' *Viaggio in Dalmazia* (1774).
28. Petrovskij, *Pervye gody*, p. 521.
29. For his review, see Grimm, *Kleinere Schriften* (1869), IV, 427–436.

writing that Vuk probably used when he was working for Karađorđe. Following the Adelung rule, "Write as you speak," he did not use the symbol *x*, because the sound it represented was absent from his dialect. Rather, he wrote: "Da li narod naš ni e nikada ni imao svoi[h] Nacionalni[h] pesana? Ili e imao i i[h] sad ima." He did not use ы or ъ (*biti, ezik*), and he used the symbol ь to indicate palatal consonants (*sadašnьi, Serblьi*). Although Vuk's orthography showed a definite attempt at simplification, and his morphology was consistent with forms of his own dialect, his Foreword retained some Russian-Slavonic lexical influences. It included a liberal sprinkling of Russian Slavonic words that he did not Serbianize, such as *blagodejaniju, otečestvo, razsuždavati, sožaleniem, razsuždavajući, tolkovati*, and *prosveščeniju*. But even with such borrowings, the morphology was Serbian.

In his "Subscription Appeal" for the forthcoming *Pismenica* Vuk repeated Kopitar's and Dobrovský's division of Serbian writers into three groups: those who wrote pure "Slavonic," those who wrote "simply Serbian (prosto Serbski)," and those who "began to write in some new language (between Serbian and Slavonic)." [30] Many years later Karadžić described to Izmail Sreznevskij the hurried approach he took to writing his first grammar: "Educating myself some more through conversations with Kopitar, and feeling all the more the need for a Serbian grammar for my own purposes, I decided to write it myself, and taking Mrazović's *Grammar* I began to rewrite the changes of nouns and verbs, correcting them into Serbian." [31] In the Foreword to the *Pismenica* Kopitar's tutoring was evident in Vuk's humble request that the reader not compare his poor grammar with the works of the immortal Adelung and Dobrovský. He repeated the Adelung rule for orthography, but modified it to: "Write as you speak; and read as it is written" (*SG*, I, 7). He disdained the mixed language of the Slaveno-Serbian school and proclaimed instead that he would give the forms used by the simple peasants "who live in the villages far from the cities."

Like Kopitar in his earlier review of *Novine Serbske*, Vuk Karadžić listed various orthographical reforms proposed by

30. Stojanović, *Život i rad V. S. Karadžića*, p. 83.
31. Quoted in Sreznevskij's sketch about Vuk, translated by Miloš Moskovljević in *Srpski književni glasnik*, 52 (1937), 391.

Obradović, Atanasije Stojković, Sava Tekelija, Pavle Solarić, Lukijan Mušickij, and Sava Mrkalj. He favored the Mrkalj system, which rejected eighteen of forty-four Slavonic letters.[32] Of the remaining twenty-six letters, he deleted ь (hitherto used in combination with *t, d, l,* and *n* to represent the Serbian palatals), and proposed the exclusive use of the old Serbian letter ħ to symbolize *ć*. Vuk also suggested three new symbols: љ, љ, њ, created by analogy to ħ, which he thought had been formed by combining *t* and ь. Like Mrkalj, Karadžić insisted that yod was a consonant; both of them used ї to represent this sound. But lapsing into the kind of etymological consideration of which Adelung and Dobrovský would have approved, Vuk reinstated *x* in his alphabet, explaining that although Serbs "have difficulty in pronouncing" this sound, it still could be written "wherever it is found in the Slavonic language . . . and in this way it could be of great use and help to us in many places" (*SG*, I, 13).

The *Pismenica* also deals with how the pitch of Serbian words is to be indicated in writing. Vuk advocated the use of diacritics in cases where confusion might arise, as between the nominative singular and the genitive plural of feminine nouns.[33] Kopitar had previously commented briefly on the necessity for marking length and pitch in Serbian. He regretted that Mrkalj had not treated the subject, and he disapproved of that writer's use of double vowels to indicate long vowels (*vooz* for *vôz*). Kopitar suggested that "pitch marks" (Tonzeichen) be employed, but only with "grammars, dictionaries, and foreign words" (*KS*, 259).

There is a parallel between Kopitar's earlier minimization of language differences among the Serbs and Croats, and Karadžić's oversimplification of the dialect situation. In the *Pismenica*, Vuk divided his language into three dialects, based on the reflex of *jat'* in each group. He applied the terms "Hercegovačko," "Sremsko," and "Slavonsko" to what later would be called "ijekavski,"

---

32. Avraam Mrazović's *Rukovodstvo* has only forty-two letters; Karadžić added ж and ѡ and mentioned that ħ and ђ were sometimes used, which would give a total of forty-six.

33. Vuk borrowed his analysis of the Serbian tonal system from Luka Milovanov of Pest (*SG*, I, 13), in whose home he had stayed while doing much of the *Pismenica*.

"ekavski," and "ikavski." He admitted no significant local differences in morphology, nor did he see any lexical problems: "And
that some call a 'devojka' a 'cura,' and others call a 'ložica' a
'kašika,' that is a small difference in dialect." This gross under-
statement, motivated perhaps by the desire to create general acceptance for the *Pismenica*, created long-range problems that have not
been solved to this day.[34]

It is ironic that the *Pismenica* is not modeled after Kopitar's
Grammatik or Dobrovský's Czech grammar, but after Avraam
Mrazović's *Rukovodstvo kъ slavenstěj grammaticě* (Guide to Slavonic
Grammar),[35] the book it was designed to replace. In their haste to
publish a grammar, Kopitar and Vuk probably decided that it was
simpler to adapt Mrazović's book than to try to digest and apply the
linguistic principles underlying the other two works. But contrary to
what Vuk told Sreznevskij many years later, he did not merely take
Mrazović's models and change the desinences. A comparison of the
two books shows that almost all the declension and conjugation
models used by him are in fact different. It is possible that he and
his mentor wanted to make the *Pismenica* as distinct from the
Rukovodstvo as they could. Vuk owed a great debt to his prede-
cessor, however, for his treatment of the parts of speech is almost
parallel to the Slavonic model, beginning on page 48 of Mrazović's
work (1811 edition). Sometimes the *Pismenica*'s definitions are almost
literal translations of Mrazović.

---

34. Ljudevit Jonke, *Književni jezik u teoriji i praksi* (1965), describes the
problem of determining and maintaining good usage, a question that continues
to plague Croatian and Serbian grammarians. Strong disagreement arises because "many readers have their own views on language and often hold to them
very stubbornly ... they have their own linguistic feeling, and they find it
difficult to accept another person's thinking about language" (p. 181). This
independence in language questions can be attributed, at least partially, to
Kopitar's and Vuk's original statements that dialect differences among the
speakers of Serbo-Croatian were so slight that everyone should write as he spoke.
Of course, the simultaneous beatification of the vernacular, achieved through the
publication of the folk songs, has led Serbs and Croats ever since to view the
vernacular and the literary language as one and the same. See Jonke, *Književni
jezik*, p. 182.

35. *Rukovodstvo kъ slavenstěj grammaticě ispravlenněj vo upotreblenie Slaveno-
Serbskihъ narodnyhъ učilištъ, izdano trudomъ Avraama Mrazoviča*. First published in 1794, this work aroused enough demand to require a fourth edition,
published in Buda in 1811, just three years before Vuk's *Pismenica*.

Kopitar's *Grammatik*, Mrazović's *Rukovodstvo*, and Karadžić's *Pismenica* were unusual for their era in that they treated verbal aspect as a separate category. In his *Grammatik* Kopitar criticized the folly of "the Russian method," which mixed different aspectual forms within the same conjugation. Kopitar's book gave two aspects —imperfective and perfective—whereas Vuk's *Pismenica* offered three: "soveršitelni, nesoveršitelni, and učešćivatelni." Karadžić's frequentative was surely an adaptation of Mrazović's "učaščatelnyj."

As a pedagogical tool, the *Pismenica* is superior to Kopitar's cluttered and pedantic *Grammatik*. Kopitar ambitiously attempted both to review the history of Slovene writing, indicating which elements of the old should be retained, and to select acceptable present-day speech forms for the new grammar. In 1814 Vuk Karadžić did not have the knowledge for an analogous historical treatment, nor was one necessary. His collaborator already knew more than any other scholar of the time about the writing of Serbs, Croats, and Slavonians ("Šokci"), had carefully studied their past lexicographical and grammatical efforts and commented on them in the Austrian press, was one of the few Slavists able to point out the more immediately Russian rather than Old Slavonic base of the Slaveno-Serbian mixtures, and had analyzed the reforms of Obradović, Solarić, Mušickij, Mrkalj, and others. It is a tribute to Kopitar's briefing of Vuk that a later Russian commentator was able to say: "The services of Vuk Karadžić in Serbian literature are not at all belittled by a recognition of the fact that his predecessors indicated all those necessary innovations which he was able to systematize and apply."[36] The fortuitous combination, dictated by necessity, of a traditional Latin format (after Mrazović) and a completely synchronic content (after Kopitar) made the *Pismenica* well suited for the use of educated people, yet comprehensible at the lowest level of literacy. It represented a good start toward the kind of normalized secular literary language advocated by Dositej in his "Letter to Haralampije," nor was it an accident that a great admirer of Obradović had inspired its creation.

Nowhere in his Dedication did Vuk Karadžić mention his sponsor's name. The omission was not owing to carelessness or ingrati-

---

tude, but was rather a matter of strategy. Kopitar knew that the Serbian Orthodox hierarchy greatly feared the efforts of a Slovene Catholic, in Austrian service, to promote a reform of their literary language. He knew that Serbs would approach Vuk's grammar more readily if his own role were unknown. He also planned to review it, in an effort to interest German linguists in this rare example of a synchronic grammar, for German approbation would enhance the book's prestige with some Vojvodina intellectuals, particularly the Austrian-educated ones. No European scholar would take Kopitar's review seriously, however, if his part in the work's conception were known.

Vuk wrote the bulk of his *Pismenica* in Pest, while Kopitar was in Paris, arranging for the return of materials stolen from the Imperial Library by Napoleon's armies.[37] When he returned, Kopitar wrote a long review, "Serbische Sprache" which appeared in the *Wiener allgemeine Literaturzeitung* in 1815 (*KS*, 310–320). His opening words boom out as though to greet a long-awaited and highly-esteemed friend: "Welcome, first Serbian grammar with Cyrillic letters! And twice welcome that you have been written faithfully after the speech of the common people!" The review is a mixture of strong praise and weak criticism. Kopitar pointed out again that the Russians, since Peter's time, had not been writing Old Slavonic but had been using some spoken Russian. Therefore Serbs should stop imitating Russian Slavonic and start writing as they spoke. Kopitar singled out twenty-five specific points, offering many helpful comments and few strictures. His remarks show how intensively he had studied Serbian and its history. His chief objection was to Vuk's three new symbols љ, љ, and њ, on the grounds that they were not simple. He suggested that the Latin *j* would be more suitable than *ï* to represent yod. The review was of course designed to support both men's radically new approach to Serbian orthography and grammar, and it was skillfully done.

Vuk's *Pismenica* at first gained few adherents and many opponents in the Vojvodina, where the ultraconservative Orthodox hierarchy still held the secular language in protective custody. But Kopitar and his protégé were unwilling to wait until the reasonableness of their

37. Miodrag Ibrovac, *Kopitar i francuzi*, p. 2.

program should win the support of Serbian writers and educators. They decided to demonstrate the superiority of their simple grammar to the "mix-it-yourself" approach by publicly ridiculing the inconsistencies of a popular writer, Milovan Vidaković, whose works Vuk had previously praised in the Foreword to his *Pjesnarica*. The critique of his novel *Usamljeni Junoša* was published in September 1815 in *Novine Serbske*, the only forum for Serbian literary discussion during its brief existence from 1813 to 1822).[38] Vuk's criticisms were blunt and undiplomatic, hardly constituting an invitation to a language congress such as he had proposed a year before in the *Pismenica*. The "Critique of *Usamljeni Junoša*" is considered the first shot in the War for a Serbian Language and Orthography, a struggle lasting several decades. Vuk's main opponents, the Slaveno-Serbs, were patriotic men who also sought a simplified, normalized grammar for Serbian education and literature. But the Vojvodina intellectuals were in awe of the Slavonic past, and they considered it a sacred duty to retain some Slavonic elements in the new Serbian literary language. To understand the Slaveno-Serbian position, and why it was so tenaciously defended for nearly half a century, it is necessary first to discuss the history of early Serbian writing.

III. SERBIAN LITERARY LANGUAGE AND ORTHOGRAPHY THROUGH THE
SEVENTEENTH CENTURY

No one has yet made the detailed studies needed for an accurate, generalized history of the Serbian literary language. The early texts are generally religious, commercial, or administrative documents, of interest to the historian but not to the literary critic. Linguists have shown an interest in them, but have yet to face certain basic problems, particularly those caused by the varying orthographical systems used. The history of Serbian writing has been complicated by the problem of foreign influences, as well as by the destruction of many

38. Although Vuk had originally written a critique of *Usamljeni Junoša* in May 1814, a month before the *Pismenica* came out, the published review did not appear until September 1815. The original text must have been somewhat revised, for specific reference is made to a page in the *Pismenica*. It would be interesting to know whether the first version maintained the humble posture of the *Pjesnarica* or the reasonable approach of the *Pismenica*. The sarcastic, imperious tone of the published review can best be explained as a reaction to the unfavorable response met by the *Pismenica* in the Vojvodina.

original documents during the frequent wars that have cursed the Serbian lands. Part of today's confusion about the nature of the early literary language stems from Vuk's polemical use of excerpts from selected manuscripts of the period 1500–1725, in order to demonstrate that his opponents were not really continuing the Serbian Slavonic tradition. With the eventual triumph of two of Vuk's theses—that the spoken language of the peasant is the only authentic Serbian, and that the language of the older manuscripts is both corrupt and only partly native—even the scholars tended to overlook orthographical and morphological peculiarities in the manuscripts and to publish texts in a normalized, "corrected" form.

A Serbian tradition of orthography and a system of morphology based on Old Church Slavonic evolved during the twelfth to the fourteenth centuries, but with numerous local variations. By the beginning of the fifteenth century the language was fairly stabilized, and the reforms of Cyril of Kostenec (Kiril Kostenečkij ca. 1380–1450), a Bulgar working at the court of Despot Stevan Lazarević, brought more order into the chief liturgical texts. He re-introduced some letters that had rightly fallen into disuse, particularly ы and ъ, and thus turned the Serbs from their native tradition toward something more like the Bulgarian-Macedonian and Russian type of Slavonic orthography. Some of his rules were too artificial to be effective, particularly the use of ы versus u and ъ versus ь; and as Đura Daničić points out, even the copyist of Kostenec's treatise "O pismenexъ" (About Letters) was unable to follow the rules and sometimes used ы where u was required, and vice versa.[39] Yet despite the ignorance of the clergy in the darkest days of the Turkish occupation and the faultiness of the copies produced by their few scribes, the general outlines of the Serbian Slavonic literary language remained fairly stable, as reflected in the printed books that began to appear at the end of the fifteenth century.

The first printed books in Slavic were in Glagolitic and were apparently the work of natives of Croatia, the very first being printed in 1483, probably at Venice. Yugoslavs were active as printers in Italy, and soon they began to produce books for their own people.[40] The first Cyrillic book, an *Oktoikh*, was printed either at Cetinje or

39. Đura Daničić, "Knjiga Konstantina filosofa o pravopisu," p. 3.
40. Josip Badalić, *Jugoslavica usque ad annum MDC*, pp. 7–13 and *passim*.

Obod in Montenegro, in 1494, apparently followed by four more by
1500. These were liturgical works in typical Serbian Church Slavonic,
expressly for the use of the Orthodox Slavs. Conditions in the Serbian
lands were extremely difficult, and in the next century most of their
printing was done in Venice, although books did appear in Goražde,
Bosnia (1520, 1521, 1531); at the monasteries of Rujno (1537),
Gračanica (1539), and Mileševa (1544, 1557); Belgrade (1552);
Mrkšina Crkva (1562, 1566); and Scutari (1563). Now if the Bosnian
books and the half-dozen Croatian Protestant translations printed in
Cyrillic during the sixteenth century are omitted, six Serbian
Slavonic books came out between 1501 and 1525, sixteen in the next
quarter-century, eighteen between 1550 and 1575, and only three in
the last quarter-century.

The first Cyrillic book for northern Slavs, a *Časoslovec* (Horo-
logium), was printed in Cracow in 1491, and some printing was done
in Byelorussia about two decades later, but not until after 1560 were
printing presses allowed in Moscow. From then on, Moscow, Lvov,
and other eastern centers turned out books in increasing quantities.

From 1508 to the end of the century, about thirty books were
published in the Rumanian lands.[41] Some scholars have been led by
the identical names of the printers, Makarije, to think that there is a
connection between the 1494 Cetinje (or Obod) *Oktoikh* and the
first Wallachian book, but Vatroslav Jagić, writing with copies of
both books before him, denied this connection.[42] The Rumanian
books, in any case, belong to a special, Bulgarian-derived linguistic
tradition with an orthography and many other fundamental features
differing from the Serbian manuscripts and printed books. They
seem to have had little influence in Serbia.

The Russian influence is quite another matter. There had been
Russian-Serbian cultural contacts from as early as the eleventh century, fostered particularly by the spread of Christianity and Slavonic
literature from the South to the East. The monasteries on Mount
Athos formed especially important links in these contacts. When
Rastko Nemanja (St. Sava) left his royal home about the year 1190
and went to Athos to become a monk, he stayed first at the Russian

41. Badalić, *Jugoslavica usque ad annum MDC*, pp. 125–130.
42. Vatroslav Jagić, "Der erste Cetinjer Kirchendruck vom Jahre 1494,"
XLIII, no. 2, pp. 5–6.

monastery of Panteleimon, according to Domentian, and "he gave much gold for the building up of the monastery."[43] Vladimir Mošin casts light on what may be a special reason for St. Sava's help to the Russians. In the eleventh and twelfth centuries Balkan Slavic manuscripts had been destroyed by the anti-Bogomil inquisition of Byzantium. With the rise of the Nemanjić dynasty at the end of the twelfth century and the establishment of autocephalic churches in the Balkans, the Nemanjići turned to the Russians for books. Mošin sees a period of Russian influence on Balkan writing "in the interval between the liberation of the Balkan Slavs from the Byzantine yoke at the end of the twelfth century and the middle of the thirteenth century, when the epoch of the Tartar yoke comes into Russia."[44] He points out that St. Sava achieved a Serbian orthographical reform based on the Russian documents, and he argues that the famous scribe Grigorii, who produced at least part of the *Miroslav Gospel* (1180–1190), could have learned his Russian-style orthography and hand in Russia as well as on Athos.

After the Tartar invasions the Russians on Athos were cut off from their homeland and depended on Serbian generosity until the end of the fourteenth century, when Serbs as well as Macedonians and Bulgars began to emigrate to Russia to escape the Turkish invasion. Their impact on Russian literature is called the second South Slavic influence, almost as important as the first wave that had brought Christianity and literacy to the East Slavs in the tenth century. A Metropolitan Kiprijan, sent to Russia in 1373 by the patriarch of Constantinople, established the church canons and monastic rules there. Another scholar claimed by the Serbs (who was most probably Rumanian, although he spent time in Serbia) is Grigorije Camblak, who became metropolitan of Kiev. The fifteenth-century Serb Pahomij Logofet has been rated "the most prolific writer of old Russia."[45]

In the sixteenth century the cultural stream began to move in the opposite direction. Both at the Serbian monastery of Hilandar on

43. Domentijan, *Životi Sv. Save i Sv. Simeona*, pp. 32–34.
44. Vladimir Mošin, "O periodizacii russko-južnoslavjanskix literaturnyx svjazej X–XV vv.," pp. 70–71.
45. Stevan Dimitrijević, "Odnošaji pećskih patrijaraha s Rusijom u XVII veku," vol. 37, p. 214.

Athos and in Serbia itself Russian manuscripts began to be imported to replace the books lost to plundering Turks. The flow of Russian written materials did not start in the eighteenth century, as is commonly believed, for there is evidence that Serbian monks were receiving Russian manuscripts as early as the middle of the sixteenth century.[46] Ljubomir Stojanović has reproduced an inscription from a manuscript given in 1549 to monks from Hilandar by a certain Kozma, in the city of Kovel' in the Ukraine.[47] In the Belgrade Theological Seminary there is a Russian Slavonic New Testament (*Tolkovoe evangelie*) that was given in 1551 in Moscow to Abbot Grigorije of the Papraća Monastery in Bosnia.[48] According to one historian Hilandar monks received books from Ivan Groznyj in 1557, "and afterwards no one returned from Russia without books." The number of surviving sixteenth-century Russian manuscripts given to Serbian monasteries is not very large, for during that century the Montenegrin printers, both at Venice and in Montenegro, were able partly to satisfy the demand for religious books. But for the seventeenth century evidence exists of a veritable stream of Serbian monks to Russia seeking alms and religious books and materials. "Thus it was recorded that monks from the monastery of Mileševa in 1638, 1647, and 1652, from Beočin in 1622, Hopovo in 1641, Krušedol in 1650, Hodoš in 1651, Studenica in 1655, Papraća in 1683, and Ravanica in 1693 received books and brought them back to their monasteries."[49]

The Serbian monks came in such numbers that by the seventeenth century all arriving clergy were held at Putivl', in the southwest Ukraine. There they awaited permission to continue on to Moscow, either by special arrangement or by presenting their charters (*žalovannye gramoty*). These gramoty gave various Serbian monasteries the right to send emissaries to Russia for alms and books, usually every five to seven years. While at Putivl', the Orthodox monks were subjected to intensive interrogation on the political situation in their countries.[50]

46. Dimitrijević, "Odnošaji," vol. 37, p. 220.
47. *Stari srpski zapisi i natpisi*, I, p. 177.
48. Ljubomir Kovačević, "Beleške i natpisi," LVI, 353–354.
49. Dimitrijević, "Odnošaji," vol. 37, p. 220.
50. Platon Kulakovskij, *Načalo russkoj školy u Serbov v XVIII v.*, bk. 2, p. 261.

The manuscript and book donations were not always unilateral. In the archives of the Ministry of Foreign Affairs in Moscow was found a communication of June 5, 1654, from Gavrilo, Serbian Patriarch at Peć, stating that he had brought with him to Moscow the following books: "Tipikъ-izbranie mnogoe otъ 34 knigъ na latinskuju eresь caregradskago patriarxa Mixaila Kavasila" and "Žitie i povĕsti svjatyxъ carej srbskixъ i patriarxovъ." Gavrilo wanted the czar to have them printed and distributed. As presents to Nikon, he brought "Svitokъ žitija vsĕxъ svjatyxъ serbskixъ arxie-piskopovъ, otkudy izyde carstvie i patriaršestvo," "Tetradi Kirilla filosofa, učitelja slavjanskago," and "Kniga Vasilija Velikago, a vъ nej napečatano tri litorgii."[51]

The participation of this same Gavrilo in the great Moscow Convocation of 1655 to correct the church books is clear evidence of the closeness between the views of Russian and Serbian clerics about the religious language. The strength of the tie between the two churches is further attested by the fact that many Serbian churchmen took up permanent residence in Russia, often receiving high positions there. Most noteworthy is Teodosije, metropolitan of Vršac, who was made an acting patriarch (*bljustitel' patriaršago prestola*) after Nikon was deposed.[52]

The degree to which Serbian monasteries and churches had become dependent on Russian Slavonic manuscripts and printed books by the first part of the eighteenth century is confirmed by a report of the Belgrade Exarch Maksim Radković, written in 1733, when Belgrade and much of Serbia were temporarily (1718–1739) under Austrian control. Radković had made a survey of the Orthodox parishes in the entire northern and northeastern part of Serbia. He was an unusually thorough reporter, not only relating his interrogations of the various priests concerning dogma, but actually reproducing his questions, their answers, and his corrections. He recorded the number of children in a priest's family, and the number of candlesticks in his church. It is probable that his description of the books possessed by each priest is accurate. Here are some samples:

51. Dimitrijević, "Odnošaji," vol. 37, p. 244.
52. Kulakovskij, *Načalo*, bk. 2, pp. 262–263.

Jerej Lazar Jovanović: "Svoja domašnija imat: popadiju i jedinu dšter na udadbu, bolše nikoga. Knigi: 1 trebnik kijevski mali; 1 liturgiju moskovskuju sa tipikom, otnel mu vladika Maksim. 1 psaltir srbski rukopis so posljedovanijem; 1 molitvoslov kijevski."

Jerej Joan Tomić: "Imat svojih knigi: 1 trebnik moskovski; 1 psaltir kijevski; časoslov kijevski; praznično evangelije i apostol lvovski; 1 časoslov grečeski."

Sveštenik pop Petar: "Knigi svoje sveštenik imejet: polustav moskovski. Psaltir moskovski; leturgija moskovska; desetoslovije moskovsko."

At the famous monastery of Ravanica, the following individuals had these collections:

Gavril, Kaluger: "Knige svoje imejet: polustav moskovski i časlovac srbski i trebnik ugrovalahiski."

Georgije Jeromonah: "Knigi svoje imejet polustav kijevski; trebnik kijevski; sabornik srbski; časlovac moskovski."

Gavril Jeromonah: "Knigi svoje imejet: polustav kijevski; trebnik kijevski; časlovac srbski."

At the monastery of Vitaonica:

"Knigi crkovni: mineja rukopisna 10, oktojiha 3, psaltira srbski pet; Evangelije okrom trapeze rukopisna dva, leturgije srbske četiri, i trebnika moskovski četiri ... jedan rukopis, molebnik jedan moskovski; sabornik srbski; biblija moskovska jedna."[53]

This highly informative report, which covers 167 modern printed pages, demonstrates beyond a doubt the great predominance of Russian printed books at the beginning of the eighteenth century in the monasteries and churches of northern and northeastern Serbia. In view of transportation difficulties, the danger of plunder by robbers and Cossack bands between Russia and Rumania, and the constant disruptions from warfare with the Turks, it is probable that such a collection could be accumulated only over a period of several decades, if not a century. Familiarity with such works had considerable influence on Serbian writing in the seventeenth and eighteenth centuries. The excerpt just quoted from Exarch Radković's report shows an abundance of Russian Slavonic forms.

53. Gavrilo Vitković, "Izveštaj, napisao 1733 g. Maksim Radković, eksarh beogradskog mitropolita," LVI, 156–180.

It is not easy to sort out the variations within the general Serbian Slavonic manuscripts and books, or the new complications introduced by imitations of the Russian texts. In characterizing the literary language of the Serbs in Hungary, Boris Unbegaun identifies it as the Serbian Slavonic that had been in use throughout the Middle Ages and "which had not changed much until the end of the seventeenth century. This language was Church Slavonic, but influenced by spoken Serbian." To illustrate, he cites a passage from a liturgical manuscript copied at about the same time as Radković's report and given to the metropolitan of Niš in 1736, which follows in part:

Цар‌ꙋ Ꙋрошꙋ. Слава. Ѿ корене царска прекрасныѧ ветавь израсте, благоꙋханни кринь, блаженни царь Ꙋрошь. Из млада возлюбивь Христа, благоименнть венценосаць биль еси, благочастнемь и верою пресветло ꙋкрашень, благꙋчастивь скиптроносаць и прензредань и пренменнть, светне тронце, милостнꙗми же и чистотою пространое селение биль еси Дꙋха светаго, еретичаскихь ꙋченн ѡбличение, церквамь светлое ꙋкрашение, вась ѿ юности Господꙋ возложиль се еси, вадови и сироти санабдевае ѡтачаски, вражди ꙋтолае и мирь ꙋтврьждае, нищнхь милꙋе, ѡбидимие изимае, достолепно царствовавь ѡтачаствн своемь.

Unbegaun comments:

> This text permits us to grasp all the essential features of Serbian Slavonic. The pronunciation is purely Serbian: the *y* is pronounced *i* (*биль*...); the distinction between hard and soft vowels does not exist ... the symbol ь, divested of any phonetic function, has only the graphic value of the ъ in modern Russian ... *ě* is pronounced and is written *e* (*ветавь, вера*, etc.); ę has become *e* ... ь and ъ in strong position have become *a* (*венценосаць*...). The frequency of ь in Slavonic words, whose Serbian equivalents gave an *a*, finished by developing among men of letters the tendency, while reading a Slavonic text, to pronounce any nonfinal ь as *a*, and to express this pronunciation in writing (no matter what the position of the ь).[54]

It is indisputable that this text shows certain features of spoken Serbian, but it would be wrong to generalize from it about the norms

54. Boris Unbegaun, *Les débuts de la langue littéraire chez les Serbes*, pp. 17–18.

of Serbian Slavonic orthography. For instance, the use of *e* for *jat'* was not typical of the early Serbian Slavonic manuscripts nor of the printed books of the fifteenth and sixteenth centuries. The substitution of *a* for a jer in weak position (*vadova, vazložil, otačaski*) was not the rule in literature, but is a "corruption" found at first chiefly in civil documents. The above text, written in 1736 and commonly known as Aleksandar's Manuscript, is particularly unsuitable as an illustration of Serbian Slavonic orthography because it contains mainly church songs, and such toparia or hymns generally had their own artificial phonetic norms.

A new type of orthography based on Serbian church pronunciation and similar to that in Aleksandar's Manuscript did arise in the seventeenth century, replacing the age-old Serbian Slavonic orthography. It seems no coincidence that this new writing system became widespread after the cessation of Serbian printing activity. It is probable that the use of printed books in Serbian monasteries and churches during the sixteenth century led to the neglect of monastic copying centers and the loss of the art of traditional Serbian Slavonic orthography. Then, after Serbian printing declined in the last quarter of the sixteenth century, Russian manuscripts and books began to be imported, and since Serbian monks had to travel long distances to get these texts and were allowed to visit Russia only periodically, it is likely that there was a compensatory resurgence of domestic copying activity. Now seventeenth-century Serbian copyists did not transpose the prominent Russian features of the imported texts into the corresponding Serbian Slavonic ones (here ignorance and practicality probably walked hand in hand), but instead they applied the norms of Serbian church pronunciation, writing, for example, the spoken *vaz-* for the Russian *voz-*, unlike their predecessors, who had for centuries written *vъz-* where *vaz-* was spoken. Thus, it was evidently in the reading and copying from Russian manuscripts and books that the Serbian church pronunciation became incorporated in a new orthography, which I will refer to as *va ime* (from the standard invocation, "In the name of the Father, and of the Son, etc.").

The contrast between the old and the new Serbian orthographies is well illustrated by some documents in Vuk Karadžić's *Primjeri srpsko-slavenskoga jezika* (Examples of the Serbian Slavonic Language).

In the left-hand column of the page he reproduces a text from a printed Serbian Slavonic book, and in the adjacent column he gives the same text from a manuscript, written in the *va ime* orthography, which he calls "Serbianized." The orthography in the printed excerpts is close to that of the earliest Serbian Slavonic manuscripts, whereas that in the Serbianized samples is like the writing in Aleksandar's Manuscript. The following are two *Credo*'s reproduced by Karadžić:

Из србуља штампанијех.
(Printed Serbian Slavonic.)

Вѣроую вь юдиного бога
wтьца вьседрьжителга, творца
нѣбѣ и земли, видимимь же
вьсѣмь и невидимимь. и вь
юдиного гда Исоуса Христа
сына божіа юдинороднаго,
ѿ отьца рожденаго прѣжде
вьсѣхь вѣкь, свѣта ѿ свѣта,
бга истиньна, рожденьна а не
сьтвореньна, юдиносоущьна
wтьцоу, имьже вьса бышє нась
ради чловѣцѣхь, и за наше
спасеніе сьшьдьшаго сь небесь.

Посрбљено из рукописа.
(Serbianized from a Manuscript.)

꙳ерꙋю ва едіного бога wца
васедржителга, творца небѕ и
земли, відімім же васем и
невідімим. і ва еднаго господа Ісѕса Хріста сина божіа
едінороднаго, ѿ wца рожденаго прежде васеꙋ векъ, света
ѿ света, бога истіна ѿ бога
истіна, рождена а несатворена,
едіносѕщна wцѕ, имже васа
бише нас ради чловецеꙋ, и
за наше спасеніе сашадшаго са
небес.

The *va ime* orthography became widespread in the second half of the seventeenth century and may be found in manuscripts as well as correspondence. It appears (albeit with some unassimilated Russian forms) in the pastoral letters of Arsenije Čarnojević, Serbian patriarch at the end of the seventeenth century. This type of writing may have reached its zenith in the unpublished works of the early eighteenth century writer Gavrilo Venclović, who was consciously trying to write in the popular language. Venclović's language indicates that the *va ime* orthography had gradually developed into a system for incorporating Russian vocabulary into a vernacular-based literary language. This orthography did not die out completely in the eighteenth century, even after the official church acceptance of Russian Slavonic. In Jovan Rajić's *Sobranie raznyhъ nedelnyhъ i pražničnyhъ nravoučitelnyhъ poučenii* (Collection of Different Sunday and Holiday Morally-Instructive Sermons), a translation of a Russian work which was published in Vienna in 1789, many Russian words were not translated but were merely transposed into Serbian, as a *va ime* scribe would have done (*aganacъ, zvezdočatacъ, zemledě-lacъ, pobědonosacъ, tajnovidacъ, nedostatakъ, bezkonačni, vanimanie, vaobražavati, vaspitati, vashytiti, prevashodstvo, saborъ, savakupiti.*) Because Rajić had studied three years at the Kiev Theological Seminary and could write comparatively well in Russian Slavonic, it is reasonable to assume that his Serbianizations were not due to ignorance, but rather that in translating for the lower clergy and general public he had taken the native *va ime* orthography and applied it to the Russian Slavonic lexicon.[55] The *va ime* literary language, which was a synthetic but native mixture of Serbian and Serbianized Slavonic, could have provided the basis for a modern Serbian literary language had it not been for certain adverse political events at the end of the seventeenth century which made it imperative that Serbia tie herself as closely as possible to Russia.

IV. ORIGINS OF THE SLAVENO-SERBIAN SCHOOL

In 1690 the Serbian patriarch, Arsenije Čarnojević III, led a mass migration of his countrymen from southern and eastern Serbia across the Danube into Hungary. The "Great Migration" (Velika Seoba) was a direct result of the Turkish victory over the Austrian and Serbian armies in 1689. First inhabitants of southern Serbia, and then those of eastern Serbia and Srem, fled in fear of the Turkish vengeance that awaited them for having supported the Austrian armies. The magnitude of this human tragedy is described by Aleksa Ivić:

In the time between the fall of Niš and the beginning of the siege of Belgrade the migration of Serbs into Hungary, headed by Arsenije, was completed. Right up to the siege of Niš the Serbian refugees in Belgrade and on the bank of the Sava had hoped that they would soon

---

55. Vuk pointed out the native elements in Rajić's language, in his article "Glavne razlike između današnjega slavenskoga i srpskoga jezika," first published in *Danica* (1826), pp. 41–69, and reprinted in *SG*, II, pp. 261–273. Aleksandar Mladenović has recently published an excellent analysis of the vernacular elements in Rajić's literary language, in his *O narodnom jeziku Jovana Rajića.*

return to their homes, but at the news that Niš was besieged and that the army ... had crossed the Danube into Erdelj, this hope disappeared, and instead of returning home, the refugees were forced to cross the Sava and to flee farther ... An indescribable panic set in among the residents of Srem and everyone hurried to reach Baranja and Bačka as quickly as possible, so that in a short time Srem was abandoned not only by the emigrants from Serbia but also by those who had permanently settled in Srem even earlier.[56]

One section of the Serbian refugees settled in the area between the Danube and Tisza rivers, in the region about Segedin, Subotica, Baja and Debrecin. A second group went further into Hungary, with some 15,000 settling in the neighborhood of Buda alone. Čarnojević was the political as well as religious leader of this group. When he crossed into Hungary, he brought with him the relics of Prince Lazar, as well as precious church materials and books. This transference symbolized the shift of Serbian political and cultural activity to the Austro-Hungarian lands. The Caesaro-papal nature of the Serbian patriarchate was then demonstrated by the fact that the Austrian emperor granted to Čarnojević the much disputed privileges of freedom of worship, church autonomy, and free election of archbishops. These rights were regarded by influential Serbs as vital to the safeguarding of national identity.

In the cultural sphere the Great Migration was destined to have great impact. The movement to the northeast brought a significant part of the Serbian population into closer contact with the cultures of two rival powers, Austria and Russia. Although the Austrians had the advantage of nearness, they developed no comprehensive program for peacefully integrating the Serbian minority until late in the eighteenth century, when they permitted the establishment of the Kurzbeck Cyrillic press in Vienna (1769) and instituted a system of public education (1774). In a real sense the eighteenth century was an age of ever-increasing Russian predominance in Serbian cultural life. Russian influence was strengthened by the new proximity of the Serbs to Russia, as well as by their concentration in larger, more accessible population centers. The chief factor favoring Russian cultural penetration, however, was the Serbian fear of Uniatization.[57]

56. Aleksa Ivić, *Istorija srba u vojvodini*, p. 296.
57. Pavle Popović, *Jugoslavenska književnost*, p. 85.

This frequently morbid anxiety runs as a leitmotif throughout Serbian cultural history of the eighteenth and nineteenth centuries. The lower clergy were barely literate (according to Exarch Radković's report, in 1733 there were only three schools in all of northeast Serbia), and clever Jesuit proselytizers often enticed the Orthodox priests into joining the Uniate church. More than half of the Serbian clergy was said to have been Uniatized during the first twenty-two years after the migration.[58]

Because of such early Austrian attempts to assimilate the Serbian nation, the Orthodox hierarchy later regarded any Austrian intrusion in its cultural life as highly suspect. For example, when the Austrian government permitted the establishment of the Kurzbeck Cyrillic press, it also decreed that all nonreligious books should be printed in the Roman alphabet, using the "simple štokavian dialect in which books were printed for the Catholics of Slavonia and Dalmatia." The Orthodox church vehemently protested this threat to its sacred alphabet, and the decree was revoked. According to Vatroslav Jagić, the Austrian attempt to introduce the Latin alphabet together with the spoken language delayed the adoption of a vernacular-based Serbian literary language: "the people, the clergy and the broad strata of society, associating the language with the script, began from this time to fear in general the introduction of the simple folk language into the schools, seeing in it something Catholic, directed against Orthodoxy. If there had not been this persecution of Cyrillic . . . the use of the popular language in the schools . . . would have prevailed much earlier than was accomplished in fact."[59] This experience helps to explain why some later scholars, like the Russians Gil'ferding and Kulakovskij, viewed the collaboration between the Catholic Kopitar and the Orthodox Karadžić as another attempt by Austria to dilute the Serbian cultural heritage by Latinizing their alphabet. The introduction of the letter *j* in Vuk's alphabet, for example, was considered a significant first step.

The Austrian threat and the Serbian fear led directly to the founding of the Russian schools at Belgrade and Karlovci during the period 1726–1737. After the Peace of Požarevac in 1718, freeing Belgrade from the Turks and placing it under Austria, the metropolitan

58. Vitković, "Izveštaj," LVI, 119.
59. Vatroslav Jagić, *Ènciklopedija*, I, 347–348.

of Belgrade, Mojsej Petrović, turned immediately to Peter the Great for funds to build churches and schools. He also asked Peter to send teachers and books, because "the Roman teachers are causing us no small trouble, creating argument and seducing . . . the uneducated." Platon Kulakovskij points up the political aspect of Mojsej Petrović's secret appeal for help, sent through the Russian consul in Vienna, and the concomitant duplicity practiced by all sides in this contest between the Latin and Orthodox cultures: "Thus the ink had not yet dried by which the agreement was signed freeing the country from the yoke of the 'infidel Hagarians' [the Turks] when the chief representative of the people freed by Austria turns secretly to the Czar of the same faith with a request for help to struggle against Catholic propaganda." [60]

Maxim Suvorov, sent by the Russian government to organize the new school, arrived in Belgrade in 1726. Kulakovskij indicates that Suvorov was not on a purely cultural mission: "Suvorov's position was all the more difficult in that he was forced to hide the fact that he was sent by the Russian government for activity among the Serbs." [61] Not only did Suvorov have to contend with the suspicions of the Austrian authorities, but he also had to struggle with the resistance of the lower Serbian clergy, who bore the burden of teaching in Serbia. Hitherto, reading had been confined to the various church books, and the students, mostly future priests, were expected to learn their selections by rote.[62] Suvorov is important because he established a degree of systematization in Serbian teaching and because he brought with him the means for normalizing writing in Serbia. His main tools were Meletij Smotrickij's *Grammatiki slavenskija pravilnoe sintagma* (A Correct Syntagma of Slavonic Grammar), first published in Vilna in 1619, the *Leksikon Trejazyčnyj* (Trilingual Dictionary) of Polikarpov (1704), and the *Bukvar'* (Primer) of Feofan Prokopovič, first published in 1721.

Smotrickij's grammar had gone through several editions during the approximately one hundred years before its influence was felt in Serbia. Like other grammatical works produced at the time, this handbook dealt not with the ancient form of Church Slavonic but

60. Kulakovskij, *Načalo*, bk. 2, p. 293.
61. Kulakovskij, *Načalo*, bk. 2, p. 238.
62. Aleksandar Jorgović, "Škole u karlovačkoj mitropoliji," IV, 666.

with the Church Slavonic of the later manuscripts and printed books. Moreover, Smotrickij, like Dobrovský and Vidaković two centuries later, tried to "correct" and "improve" the language. For example, he eliminated the double negative (precisely one of the "improvements" for which Vuk would criticize Vidaković). Jagić asserts that the Smotrickij grammar underwent extensive revision in the 1648 Moscow edition. Probably this revision did much to promote the mistaken eighteenth-century Serbian conception that Russian Slavonic and the Old Church Slavonic literary language were one and the same. Smotrickij himself had been able to distinguish Russian from Old Slavonic forms. In the Vilna edition of 1619 he had translated certain Greek figures of speech into both Slavonic and Russian, but in 1648: "The Muscovite editor, having no feeling for the West-Russian dialect, did not allow the idea that there existed between Slavonic and 'Russian' any kind of distinction." [63] As a matter of fact, the Moscow editor was perpetuating an old error that came originally from the South. The South Slavic languages, particularly Bulgarian and Macedonian, had evolved so rapidly from the eleventh to the fourteenth centuries that the general feeling of kinship with the Old Church Slavonic texts was often lost. Even Cyril of Kostenec, and therefore probably his teacher, Euthymius of Trnovo, believed that the "corrupt" language of the late fourteenth-century manuscripts did not go back to a real Bulgarian but was an artificial language, whose chief and "purest" component was Russian.[64] This view of the primacy of Russian elements in Slavonic was zealously cultivated by the Russians.

The Moscow edition of Smotrickij's grammar was further edited in the eighteenth century and republished in 1721 and 1755 by Polikarpov and in 1723 by Maksimov. Thus, the grammar that Suvorov brought with him to Belgrade in 1726 reflected the norms of a literary language first established a century earlier and then modified according to the character of the hybrid Kievan-Moscovite Russian Church Slavonic in the early eighteenth century. In 1755 this book was republished in full at Rimnik in Wallachia, at the request of the Serbian Archbishop Pavel Nenadović. In 1794 a condensed version was brought out by Avraam Mrazović, which was reprinted

63. Jagić, *Ènciklopedija*, I, 31.
64. See chapter on Kostenečki in Vasil Kiselkov, *Prouki*, esp. pp. 284–285.

a number of times, the last edition appearing in 1811. (Since Vuk's *Pismenica*, published in 1814, borrowed much from Mrazović's work, it can be said to trace its lineage back to Smotrickij.)

That the language taught in the Serbian schools set up by Suvorov and his replacement, Emanuilo Kozačinskij, and continued by their Serbian successors, was basically the Russian literary language of the first part of the eighteenth century may also be seen in the fact that the *Bukvar'* used was that written by Prokopovič in 1721. According to its Foreword, the book was written at the direction of Peter the Great, to give a clear explanation of "God's law and the Creed and the Lord's Prayer and the nine beatitudes." Since it was to be used in teaching the young to read, Peter decreed that it be written "not in the high Slavic dialect" (slavenskim vysokim dialektom) but "in the vernacular" (prostorečiem).[65]

Serious problems faced eighteenth-century Serbs trying to master Russian Slavonic as a literary language, for there were now apparently three styles of pronunciation, which might be characterized as *vo imja*, reflecting the Russian orthography, *va ime*, or the typical Serbian church pronunciation for both domestic manuscripts and imported Russian books, and *u ime*, the spoken language of the uneducated masses. The last variety intruded into the written language of an intellectual in inverse proportion to his sophistication in the Russian Slavonic. In spite of the establishment of Suvorov's school, it was difficult for the eighteenth century Serb to remain aware of the interrelationships among the various styles of speaking and spelling. With such difficulties in mind, Zaharije Orfelin published a primer (about 1764), basing it on Prokopovič's work.[66] Orfelin's book was an attempt to simplify the learning process, in the best tradition of eighteenth century rationalism, by teaching Serbs to pronounce Russian Slavonic correctly from the start, thereby eradicating the *va ime* pronunciation. In his Foreword Orfelin wrote:

> Experience itself shows that Serbian children learning to read Slavonic books lose much time in the beginning and consequently not many leave school who can read correctly and well without error;

65. Kulakovskij, *Načalo*, bk. 3, p. 283.
66. *Pervoe učenie hotjaštyimъ učitisja knigъ pismeniy slavenskimi, nazyvaemoe bukvarъ.*

this is because they do not have fundamental teaching in the very beginning. It is true that they use Moscow primers less and Kievan more, but these are made for Russians, to whom the pronunciation of Slavonic letters and words is natural, and who also have teachers who are . . . more capable, while it is just the opposite with the Serbs, where the pronunciation of words is completely strange . . . and thus these primers are not of much use to Serbian children.

Orfelin criticized Serbs who in their pronunciation transposed *vo imja* into *va ime*, the letter *o* into *a*, and the letter *ja* into *e* (from Common Slavic ę) and who omitted the sound *h* in pronunciation.[67] Orfelin also excoriated those who pronounced *jat'* as *e*, and words like *plot* as *plt*. Accepting the Moscow-Russian pronunciation of the symbol щ as *šč* (the true Slavonic pronunciation should be *št*, as Vuk later pointed out in the *Primjeri*) Orfelin failed to distinguish the difference between the Russian palatalized consonants *tь*, *dь*, and *lь*, and the Serbian palatals *ć*, *đ*, and *lj*, and he recommended that these Russian palatalized consonants be given the pronunciation of the Serbian palatals.

Orfelin's striving to inculcate the Russian Slavonic pronunciation in Serbian teaching was merely a logical result of the general belief, both inside and outside Serbia, that the Russian Slavonic literary idiom was the direct heir of the language of Cyril and Methodius. This view was not confined to Orthodox Slavdom; Rafailo Levaković and other Croat Catholics who had worked on the revision of the Croatian Glagolitic liturgy in the seventeenth century relied particularly on Uniatized Russians as well as on Russian Slavonic books. Even Dositej Obradović, who desired to relegate Russian Slavonic to a strictly religious function, believed that this language was a direct continuer of the Old Church Slavonic tradition. He wrote: "The mother language of all these nations is Slavonic, which in prosperous Russia has been brought to the highest perfection . . . all the high arts and sciences are published in it."[68]

The Serbian acceptance of Russian Slavonic also had a certain linguistic justification; indeed, several features that spoken Serbian shared with this literary idiom had already disappeared from the

67. Quoted from Dimitrije Ruvarac, "O prvom štampanom slovenskom bukvaru za srpsku decu," pp. 278, 282.
68. Dositej Obradović, *Dela*, p. 237.

spoken Russian language. For example, both spoken Serbian and Russian Slavonic used the aorist and imperfect tenses, which had long ago been lost to native Russian. In the realm of vocabulary, partly because of the increased prestige of Balkan-Slavic forms taught by scholars in the Second South Slav wave during the fifteenth and sixteenth centuries, Russian Slavonic did not reflect the native Russian pleophony but rather affected the metathesized forms that were native to Serbian, for example Common Slavic *gordъ, Russian Slavonic gradъ, spoken Serbian grâd, but spoken Russian gorod [górət].[69]

It is hard to distinguish this Russian Slavonic period of Serbian from the Slaveno-Serbian period that followed. Boris Unbegaun, whose purpose was to describe the literary language of eighteenth century Serbia, gives the following guideline:

> One can talk of a mixture only by starting from the notion of style, for from the linguistic point of view one can detect almost always either a Serbianized Slavonic, or a Slavonized Serbian, and the cases are rare where we have to deal with a true mixed language. This schema is disturbed by two complementary factors: on the one hand, Slavonic itself did not stay the same during the whole eighteenth century: it appears to us at first like a Serbian Slavonic, which later gives way to a Russian Slavonic; on the other hand, what is called Russian Slavonic is more often only a Slavonized Russian.[70]

Concentration on the element of style does not help much to clarify the problem. The presence or absence of dative absolutes, an occasional dual, or an instrumental plural in y does not tell us enough about the language of an individual author. Such considerations as the choice of vocabulary (where both a Russian Slavonic and a Serbian word are available) or the use of a Russian Slavonic or Serbian morphology are more important in establishing the type of language a writer used. Further, it is often difficult to "bracket" a writer, for like Rajić, he may write some texts in Russian Slavonic, while writing others in a *va ime* idiom. Unbegaun explained such a

---

69. Spoken Serbian also shared with "high style" Russian, the retention of the results of the progressive ("Baudouin de Courtenay") palatalization, whereby Common Slavic *k*, *g*, and *x* had changed to *c*, *dz*, and *s*. See Viktor Vinogradov, *Očerki*, p. 65.

70. Unbegaun, *Les débuts*, pp. 14–15.

flexibility in terms of function; that is, if the author is writing of the history of the Slavs, he selects what he considers the highest style, Russian Slavonic, as he knows it. If he is writing a book of sermons for the use of ignorant local priests, he selects *va ime*, a mixture of Serbianized Russian and real, spoken Serbian. But the fact is that it was not easy for a man to be perfectly at home in both *va ime* and Russian Slavonic. Although it was simple to effect a stylistic flavor by using the dative absolute or a genitive singular in *ago*, it was very difficult to shift accurately to the whole range of correct morphological forms.

Morphological consistency required more thorough training than most Serbs received toward the end of the eighteenth century. Except for those who spent periods of study or work in Russia, such as Rajić and Stojković, it was difficult for the Serbian intellectual to learn thoroughly the Russian Slavonic language. The Vojvodina Serb, if he was fortunate, studied at Catholic or Protestant lycées and gymnasia where the main languages taught were Latin and German. Metropolitan Stratimirović, for example, received his gymnasium education at the Piarist Fathers' school in Segedin.[71] The general difficulty of mastering Russian Slavonic, plus rationalism's doctrine of education for the masses (to whom that language was incomprehensible), were precisely the factors that drove Serbian intellectuals to search for another solution toward the end of the eighteenth century. Kopitar was not alone in his disgust at the varying mixtures of language being used by Serbian writers. It can safely be stated that every Serbian writer who stands out in this period must have been aware of the language problem and had ideas for alleviating it, although not all expressed their theories explicitly. There were a few extremists at both ends such as Vuk advocating a purely popular language and Pavle Kengelac favoring a complete acceptance of Russian Slavonic, but most writers seem to have been moderates, who sought to "correct" their spoken language by retaining the particular features of Russian Slavonic that they individually espoused. Their mixed but predominantly vernacular language was called Slaveno-Serbian. A very popular writer of the Slaveno-Serbian school was Milovan Vidaković, known as "the

---

71. Jovan Radonić, *Slike iz istorije i književnosti*, p. 304.

father of the Serbian novel." It was his misfortune to put his theories on language into print at about the same time that Vuk was beginning to write and to promulgate Kopitar's ideas.

V. THE VUK–VIDAKOVIĆ DEBATE

Milovan Vidaković was born in May 1780 in the village of Nemanikuća, in the Kosmaj area of Serbia. When he was nine, his family moved to Irig in the Srem region of the Vojvodina, because of the outbreak of hostilities between an Austro-Russian alliance and the Turks in the war of 1788–1791. Milovan, still illiterate, started school at Irig and went on to Segedin and Novi Sad. His education was much the same as Kopitar's in Ljubljana, involving the traditional study of Latin and Greek classics in a modern atmosphere of rationalism. The new spirit was known as "Dositejism" among the Serbs of the Vojvodina, after Dositej Obradović, the critic of the Serbian Orthodox Church. His views had been espoused by most intellectuals but were bitterly opposed by the caesaro-papal Orthodox hierarchy, especially after the accession of Stefan Stratimirović as metropolitan in 1790. Pavle Popović outlines Dositejism thus:

What he [Dositej] wrote and preached became common property, the spirit of the times. With his common-sense writings he opened the way to enlightenment, literature, and national education, and the whole of Serbian society in the Hungary and Austria of that time followed the slogans he gave. "Education, education, that is what we need," was the constant motto from then on; education in all its forms: schools, printing houses, books . . . Literature is the most important, it needs the most help; it spreads education more freely and directly than the public school, especially the Latin schools that Serbian students were attending at the time . . . Every educated man and patriot must help literature; everyone who can write usefully must write, because that is what the people especially need.[72]

The desire to help the Serbian people was the motive that Milovan Vidaković gave for writing his first work, a biblical adaptation called *Istorija o prekrasnom Iosifě* (The Story About Beautiful Joseph). In the dedication to this novel in verse, first published in 1805, the Kosmaj peasant's son wrote: "It being that common sense demands

72. Pavle Popović, *Milovan Vidaković*, pp. 9–10, 23, 24.

from us that each one, as much as his God-given strength and talent permit, should be of use in some way to his fellow man, and especially to his race, from such an obligation I, loving my Serbian race, compose for the youth this *Story About Beautiful Joseph* in verses." [73] Between this story and his work of major linguistic significance, *Ljubomir u Elisiumu*, Vidaković published two other novels, *Usamljeni Junoša* and *Blagovonnyj krin cĕlomudrennyja ljubve, libo stradatelnaja povĕst' Velimira i Bosil'ki* (The Sweet-Scented Lily of Virginal Love, or the Painful Story of Velimir and Bosilka). They are sentimental adventure novels based on German sources, which ultimately stem from Greek adventure novels written between the second and fifth centuries A.D. Heroes with fanciful names such as Tihomil', Kolumbin, Nikodim, Ljubivoj, Velimir, and Bosiljka travel to far-flung places like Russia, Constantinople, the Holy Mountain (Athos), Varna, and Egypt. Jovan Skerlić's commentary on Vidaković's craftsmanship seems especially applicable to these early works: "Vidaković is a writer of weak originality, and his novels are not only modeled on popular ... chivalric tales and philosophical-pedagogical novels, but they often are simple re-workings, Serbianizations." Vidaković was nevertheless the most widely read Serbian novelist of his day: "In the first decades of the nineteenth century there were ... people who tried to live and speak like the heroes of his novels, young writers learned how to write from him ... and parents gave their children the names of the characters in his novels." [74]

In 1814 in Buda, Vidaković published *Ljubomir u Elisiumu, Part I*. Like his previous novels, this was an adventure story, with the usual sentimental, moral-didactic digressions. The volume is remarkable, however, for its twenty-page introductory essay, "Observation on the Serbian Language," dated October 1813. The opening statement suggests that the author was not unaware of the articles on the Serbian literary language published by Kopitar in the German press: "Now we who begin to write a little for our people find ourselves in rather unpleasant times: they criticize us more for our language than for our work, but they are right too; it is the duty of the translator, as well as the writer himself, to pay as much attention to his language

73. Popović, *Milovan Vidaković*, p. 24.
74. Jovan Skerlić, *Istorija nove srpske književnosti*, pp. 147, 149.

as to the thing he is expressing in it."[75] Vidaković seemed to fall in line with Obradović and Kopitar when he wrote, in words similar to those shortly to be used by Vuk in the Introduction to the *Pjesnarica*: "Where would we get such a grammar, which would contain the pure properties of the Serbian language and would have rules that all could follow uniformly? We must be eternally grateful to Mr. Mrazović for the Slavonic grammar, but we still need a Serbian one too. And until we have this, we cannot write correctly and uniformly, but will always stray, and some will write as they speak in Srem, another as in Slavonia, and a third as in Croatia, etc."

Vidaković cited Dobrovský's three-fold grouping of Serbian writers: "A certain Dobrovský ... writes that we Serbs at present do not have a correct and defined language in which we can write books, but some of us write in church style, others simply as we speak, or mixed!" Vidaković antedated Karadžić by a few months in his appeal for a cooperative effort by educated Serbs to compose a grammar, "the first foundation on which our education ... could be based." Like Kopitar, Vidaković adhered to Dositej's conception of a clear separation between the functions of the church language and the secular literary language. He advocated keeping "our old Slavonic language" for religious books and works of interest to "learned and lofty people." As for the vernacular he asked: "Who doesn't read gladly our blessed Dositej? Both the small and the great, the old and the young, read his works gladly and with pleasure, and they profit from them, because everyone understands what is said in a book of his." Vidaković attacked the egoism of the learned minority who insisted on writing in Russian Slavonic, a language that the common man could not understand. "We need to be generous and to work for the welfare of our people, and not prejudiced [against the vernacular] just because we want to show people that we know Slavonic and can write high style, so that only learned people can understand us." Vidaković's argument for using the vernacular was as convincing as Kopitar's, but he wrote without the Censor's characteristic mockery and ridicule: "My dear readers! Although we originate from the Slavs we are no longer what we were before, but Serbs; we have our own language, which we cannot destroy, nor

75. The "Observation" is not paginated.

can we transform ourselves into Slavs again; and why would we want that? —Why don't the Italians and the French return to the Latin language . . . ?"

In an age when modern linguistic chauvinism was just beginning, Kopitar was the ultimate purist among Slavists. In his review of *Novine Serbske* he had criticized the young newspaper for "Slavonisms," pointing out that many such expressions were really native Russian. Vidaković, too, wished to "purify [Serbian] of foreign words, and to introduce our own words," but he regarded Turkish, Hungarian, and German as the alien influences. He welcomed Slavonisms, however, as an integral part of the Serbian lexical store, at which fateful point his linguistic program veered sharply away from Kopitar's. Vidaković's acceptance of Slavonic as an etymological basis was in line with the theories of Adelung and Dobrovský and the practices of Dositej Obradović. Dositej had not believed that Russian Slavonic philosophical or scientific terminology needed to be Serbianized before it could be used. Indeed, he regarded the *va ime* orthography as ignorant and "low class," the language of partly educated rural churchmen. The "corrective" influence of the eighteenth century schools of Suvorov and Kozačinskij, reinforced later by the publication of native tools for the teaching of Russian Slavonic, such as Orfelin's *Bukvar'* and Mrazović's *Rukovodstvo*, the almost exclusive use of Russian texts, and finally the general, centuries-old ignorance of the differences between high-style Russian and the language of the earliest Slavic texts, all had contributed to the universal acceptance of that imported language as pure Slavonic. Dositej's own apology for vernacular-based writing, his "Letter to Haralampije," is sprinkled with Russian Slavonic words.[76]

Kopitar, however, like his friend Humboldt, was firmly convinced that spoken languages had no gaps or inadequacies. Whereas Adelung and Dobrovský had recognized the role of etymology in creating new words, restoring old ones, or deciding which of several spoken variants should be selected for literature, Kopitar took the

76. In his "Letter to Haralampije" Obradović wrote (note the Russian Slavonicisms): "Samo prostota i glupost zadovoljava se vsegda pri starinskom ostati. Zašto je drugo Bog dao čoveku razum, rasuždenije i slobodnu volju nego da može rasuditi, raspoznati i izabrati ono što je bolje? A šta je drugo bolje nego ono što je poleznije? Što god ne prinosi kakovu libo polzu, ne ima nikakve dobrote u sebi." *Dela*, p. 4.

command *write as you speak* without the practical Adelungian quali-
fications accompanying it, such as "closest proved derivation,"
"best general pronunciation," and "common usage." A linguistic
radical, Kopitar was convinced that if people did write exactly as
they spoke, "the rest would take care of itself," as it had, he claimed,
with the ancient Greeks. Vidaković's objections in the "Observation"
to such a linguistic anarchy seem to have been directed specifically
against Kopitar's program, for as a typical Vojvodina intellectual,
he knew German well and probably had read at least a few of the
Austrian publications to which Kopitar contributed. Like Nikolaj
Trubeckoj a century later,[77] Vidaković believed it disadvantageous
for a literary language to adhere closely to a single dialect and to
reflect exclusively the speech of a writer's region:

> Nowhere are we going to find an area of the land where the people
> speak so purely and so correctly that we can take their dialect for the
> literary language. Serbs in other regions pronounce many words
> badly, like us, which the writer must correct—just as the Germans
> don't observe how their people generally speak and then write that
> way, but they write as the nature of the language informs them.
>   Nor is it worthwhile to write . . . as even the simplest people speak,
> because in every province they speak differently. Consequently, the
> writers in every region would have to write books differently. Then,
> when our Sremac would read a book that was written in Croatian, he
> would laugh because some words, to which he is unaccustomed,
> would sound strange to his ears.

Vidaković's objections to the "every man to his own dialect"
approach evinced a consciousness of the realities of human speech
not discernible in Kopitar's theories. Like the majority of Serbian
intellectuals, Vidaković wanted a linguistic amalgam based heavily
on spoken Serbian. First, he would free his native language of all
non-Slavic impurities; then he would borrow from literary, high-
style Russian wherever the proper Serbian words were lacking. As
with other European languages, the orthography should "correct"
the mistakes of "quick speech (*skori izgovor*)"—substituting, for
example, *er* where today's standard Serbo-Croatian has only
vocalic *r* (*vrh* would be written *verh*). Russian Slavonic would be the
guide. Having lived the first nine years of his life in Turkish-held

---

77. Nikolai Trubeckoj, *The Common Slavic Element in Russian Culture.*

Serbia, Vidaković lacked respect for the patois of his current home. He was certain that Vojvodina *ekavian* (*mleko, dete,* etc.) was a newer linguistic phenomenon, and that *ijekavian* (*mlijeko, dijete*) was true old Serbian. Living in the ekavian areas of Srem, Bačka, and Banat for twenty-five years put him at a disadvantage, however, as he tried to remember which words had *je* and which had *ije,* and like the copyist of Cyril of Kostenec's treatise on correcting medieval Slavonic, Vidaković gave several incorrect examples. Like Vuk, he was a patriot, and although he recognized that the center of Serbian culture was now in the ekavian Vojvodina, he still wanted to incorporate the ijekavian pronunciation in the new literary language: "Our whole people even today in those lands that our ancestors ruled for hundreds of years, and from which we came ... speak all these words purely or, here and there, with very slight change. We are convinced, therefore, that it is our real old Serbian language which our people speak from central Serbia to Macedonia, in all of Bosnia, Herzegovina, Albania, Montenegro, and Dalmatia.' Vidaković oversimplified the Serbian dialect situation, although not nearly so much as did Kopitar and Vuk.

Vidaković's "Observation on the Serbian Language" may perhaps be regarded as a representative expression of the majority viewpoint on the new national literary language, for indeed he was always a popularizer and not an original thinker. It was obvious from his statements in the essay that he and others were moving towards a vernacular-based literary language. It was highly unfortunate, therefore, that Vuk Karadžić, who had been stung by the recent Vojvodina criticism of his *Pismenica,* decided to ridicule the Slaveno-Serbs by attacking the language of their most popular author, Vidaković himself. Karadžić did not select for criticism the novelist's most recent work, *Ljubomir u Elisiumu,* but an early novel, *Usamljeni Junoša,* whose flaws Vidaković had already admitted in the "Observation," when he wrote: "Someone may say to me ... 'and why didn't you pay attention to accuracy of language in your works published up to now?'—Just as I didn't pay much attention in my early works, so ... from now on I will truly pay attention."

Vuk's motive in reviewing *Usamljeni Junoša* was apparent from the fact that he gave a few lines to praising it for its historical references, made no mention at all of its plot, and immediately began to examine the "purity" of its language: "As far as the purity and individuality of the language is concerned, there is evidence in many places that the author was born in Serbia; and in some places it is evident that he left there in his childhood, and learning foreign languages . . . he forgot his own; therefore, the reviewer ventures to make the following observations about language" (*SG*, I, 82). Vuk seemed almost to be repeating the opening remarks of Vidaković's "Observation on the Serbian Language" when he stated that it is the author's duty "to take as much care about the purity and individuality of his language as he does about his subject." A writer should be governed by the "constant rules" of his language, and since the Serbian rules were not yet "collected," authors should follow the "pure and uncorrupted speech of the Serbian people." He cited the learned German linguist Adelung: "Adelung's dictionary, and all his grammars, are nothing else except the laws of the German language collected from the German people." This comment was indeed a gross simplification, if not an actual distortion.

Vuk introduced his specific criticisms of Vidaković's writing with an ominous warning of the kind that a village priest might use to a recalcitrant youth: "That Serbian writer who sins against the speech of his people sins against the rules of his language. Here are Mr. Vidaković's mistakes" (*SG*, I, 82). The major errors he found were:

(1) Use of Russian forms, such as *ispolnenyj, polno*, instead of the Serbian forms: *ispunjeni, puno*. Karadžić also twitted Vidaković for inconsistency, in that he occasionally used Serbian forms like *dužnost* instead of the Russian *dolžnost'*.

(2) Use of the instrumental plural ending *-ami* instead of the native Serbian *-ama*.

(3) Omission of the ending for the locative plural, which Karadžić called "dative," in such expressions as *po šuma, po dubrava*.

(4) Use of the Russian Slavonic forms *sy, suštь*, instead of the Serbian *budući*.

(5) Use of the Russian Slavonic ending *-ovъ* for the genitive plural masculine: *časovъ, gradovъ, trudovъ*.

(6) Use of the instrumental singular ending *-omъ* with feminine nouns of the *bolest* type: *bolestiomъ* instead of *bolešću*.

Karadžić also pointed out that Vidaković had frequently used the incorrect ending -*u* for the third person present of *i*-stem verbs, instead of the now standard -*e*; for example, *radu, srazuse* [*srazu se*], *poletu, vodu,* and *govoru.* He declared that such an error was common among the townsfolk in the Vojvodina. Another feature noted by the reviewer was the proliferation of third plural present forms ending in *du*: *možedu, voledu,* and *boledu,* instead of *mogu, vole,* and *bole.*

Vuk made few comments on Vidaković's syntax. His overall "corrections", grammatical and syntactical, were not extensive, and his disagreements with the novelist sometimes reflected the contrast of two dialects. But his remarks produced a disproportionately intense and far-reaching reaction, for he had assumed the position of censor for a language that he himself admitted was yet to be codified. The dogmatic rigidity and lapses into sarcasm, reminiscent of his teacher Kopitar, were hardly in keeping with Adelung's conception of the grammarian: "not the lawgiver of a people, but only the collector and publisher of the laws made by them." For example, referring to Vidaković's use of phrases like *ovomu se ime* (this one's name is) and *Kako ti se ime?* (What is your name?) Vuk wrote: "This is a really disgusting thing in the Serbian language! It would be a scandal to hear it even from a Greek who is learning Serbian, to say nothing of reading it in Serbian books." In his critique he used such authoritative expressions as: "Serbs say," "Serbs don't say," and "A Serb would say this." Referring to a Vidaković weakness, he remarked: "These are all Slavonic endings, which harmonize with Serbian words like a goose with a pig." Comments such as, "The most consistent rule on this is in the *Grammar* of Mr. Vuk Stefanović on page 87," did not endear the anonymous reviewer to the novelist later, when his identity became known. That Vuk had overstepped the usual critical bounds of the day is made clear by Ljubomir Stojanović: "The critique created a real sensation among the reading public, because it was the first occasion that a writer was criticized, publicly, in the newspapers."

The question of the authorship of the review requires comment. There is reason to believe that it was coauthored, and that Kopitar wrote those parts not pertaining directly to the Serbian language. Both Nestor Petrovskij and Ljubomir Stojanović see Kopitar's direct hand in it. Stojanović quotes an entire passage of the "Introduction": "Въ прочемъ, što se raznyhъ namĕrenija savršenogъ Romana tiče, vnutreně cěne něgove, blagovkusnogъ kroja, i sojuza sviju častii kъ ednomъ ili dvoma glavnymъ naměrenijama, silnyhъ i čistyhъ figura, plodonosnogъ voobraženija, Karaktera lica dějstvujućegъ, stanja i položenija něgovogъ, običaja, zemlě, lěta i pr. ne možemo se ovde u duboko upustiti." He comments: "Such a conception of the novel could not have come from Vuk's head either in this period or later, and not even the style is Vuk's . . . This whole section can be translated into German word for word, and with the same order of words, in such a manner that a pure German sentence would result."[78] Kopitar's presence is also felt in the now imperious, now condescending attitude of the reviewer. The general flavor is the same as that of Kopitar's critiques of Rumanian and Greek books, as for example, where the reviewer writes: "We recommend that he read good novels in foreign languages" (*SG*, I, 82).

A month after the appearance of the review, Vidaković published a "Reply" in *Novine Serbske*, together with a note from the editors expressing their hope that the literary debate then beginning would soon lead to a common literary language—a forlorn hope, as it turned out, since this struggle, in various forms, was to last almost a half-century. Vidaković opened his reply with a complaint against the "pedagogical tone (tonъ učitelskii)" of his unknown critic, and he pointed out that he had disowned the language of such works as *Usamljeni Junoša* a year earlier, in his "Observation on the Serbian Language." But whereas in that essay the novelist had glibly predicted a literary language that would be "just above the language of the kitchen," he was more conservative in his "Reply," and he now introduced *class usage* as a criterion for acceptability: "I think that these words sound more beautiful and more pleasant not only to my ears but to those of every educated Serbian citizen, than his . . . ispunjen . . . puno . . . dužnostь, duga, etc. as they speak in the kitchen (*SG*, I, 89). In his "Observation" Vidaković had patriotically proclaimed his intention to restore to the literary language the ijekavian pronunciation which still prevailed in much of Turkish-held Serbia, because he believed it to be the original Serbian pronunciation. Now, he looked down his nose at that region, and remarked that he could not understand why his nameless critic compared the language of

---

78. Stojanović, *Život i rad V. S. Karadžića*, pp. 147–148; Petrovskij, *Pervye gody*, p. 708.

educated Serbs in the Vojvodina with that of their countrymen "from those lands where there are no schools, and where there is no education." Vidaković conceded that the backwoods peasant might know a few terms that the townsman would not, "something or other concerning the plow and the wagon, plus the names of some plants unknown to us," but he asked whether such peasants had the native vocabulary to talk about "the natural sciences" and "philosophy." For these subjects, Vidaković claimed, it would be necessary to borrow Russian Slavonic terminology, but he made it clear that he regarded such borrowing as a temporary stage, analogous to that which other European languages had experienced during their early development: "The lucky Germans! In the beginning of their enlightenment they were not ashamed . . . to take both Latin and French words which are beautiful and to mix them in their own language, until they had opened the hearts of their people to sweet sciences, and then . . . they began to purify their language; and now we see to what perfection they have brought it" (*SG*, I, 90).

Vocabulary is an area where the early nineteenth-century Slaveno-Serbs are least understood and most unjustly maligned. With practically no secular literary tradition behind them, men like Milovan Vidaković were trying to create a modern Serbian literature, either by translating or adapting popular European works of the late eighteenth and early nineteenth centuries and by writing original works in genres new to the Serbian language, such as the novel. It is easy to understand Vidaković's bewilderment at Vuk's contention that Serbs in the Hungarian towns did not know Serbian, for it was precisely in those places that a new literary language was evolving.

The lack of an adequate Serbian vocabulary, combined with the widespread belief that literary Russian was the direct continuer of the Old Slavonic language, helps to explain why Serbian writers were induced to mix spoken Serbian with written Russian. This procedure was similar to the one Nikolaj Trubeckoj describes as having produced the modern Russian literary language. But Trubeckoj refers to a gradual, organic fusion of Church Slavonic and spoken Russian, whereas the Slaveno-Serbian (really Russian-Serbian) wedding was artificially stimulated and hastily performed. Educated Serbs realized that the cultural situation was inadequate for a speedy solution to their language problem, but they also felt that the nearly total illiteracy of the Serbian people and the need for mass education justified speed at the expense of selectivity and condoned individual experimentation with language, even though the requisite linguistic knowledge was universally lacking. There was no single Serbian authority; and consequently, violent personal antagonisms were probably inevitable. Indeed, recent world events remind one that language is an emotionally charged and highly subjective area of human culture.[79] Vuk Karadžić's simple solution of temporary linguistic autonomy for every writer willing to adhere to the peasant's speech could hardly win an experienced novelist like Vidaković, who worried that a pungently local language might be more a cause for humor than for serious attention. A dialect-based literary language might give *form* precedence over *content*, and its very regionalism might deprive a work of universality.

VI. THE VUK–VIDAKOVIĆ DEBATE CONTINUED

Part II of *Ljubomir u Elisiumu* was printed in Buda in 1817, about two years after the initial skirmish between Vidaković and the Vienna forces. Vuk's startling attack on the well-known novelist and Vidaković's lame defense had been widely discussed within the educated Serbian circles of Austria and Hungary by readers of *Novine Serbske*. People chose sides, for intellectuals were vitally concerned with the language problem that had so long been an obstacle to national progress. Vidaković found that his strongest support came from Metropolitan Stratimirović and the church, which had suspected Kopitar's intentions from his earliest activities in Vienna.

In the Foreword to *Ljubomir, Part II*, a more confident Vidaković

---

79. Even if one excludes the example of such distant countries as India ("Linguistic fanaticism is today a much greater danger than religious frenzy"— K. Santhanam, *Transition in India and Other Essays* (Bombay, 1964), p. 68), or of closer countries such as Belgium with its Dutch-French riots, one need only point to the 1967 protests of leading Croatian writers and scholars that their language was being "Serbianized." The strong link between language and religion was underlined by the 1966 protests of Roman Catholic traditionalists in the United States against the substitution of English for Latin in the liturgy of the Mass.

counterattacked with a program for language autonomy as anarchic as the vernacular dialect proposal of Kopitar and Vuk.[80] The novelist still reserved the Slavonic for religious books and learned works, but for moral and educational writing he now proposed a compromise: "I say that we should select some middle way (sredni put) between our Serbian dialect and Slavonic, the root language" (*SG*, I, 114). This "middle way" was substantially different from the route he had earlier proposed in the "Observation," where he recommended a literary language that would differ little from "kitchen" talk and would use Slavonic primarily as a lexical source. The new proposal involved the total weaving together of Slavonic and the vernacular, including their grammar and vocabulary. Vidaković's *sredni putnik* is like a gardener who will forever walk between two language beds, selecting words, clichés, and desinences at will, each trip creating a new bouquet for his public. The novelist mentioned that he had discussed his proposal with learned men and had even received an opinion from "Mr. Dobrovský, famous philologist, and a man most skilled both in the old Slavonic language and in all its dialects." He quoted a paragraph from Dobrovský's answer, written in German: "I have now read the Critique [by Karadžić] and your answer. If I may venture an opinion, it will not be at all suitable if the Serbs should stoop to peasant speech. There must also be a higher language for more lofty subjects. A *stylus medius* (srednij slog), a middle way, should be found which would be close to the old liturgical, and also partly to the vernacular" (*SG*, I, 115). Evidently Vidaković, who had referred to the Czech in his "Observation on the Serbian Language" as "a certain Dobrovský (neki Dobrovský)," had come to appreciate the vital role that the linguist could play in supporting his position against Vuk. Conservatives such as Stratimirović and Atanasije Stojković were aware of the similarity between their general views and Dobrovský's, particularly with respect to "correcting" the spoken language for literary purposes. Throughout the Slavic world at this time Dobrovský was looked upon as a kind of detached Olympian authority. His imprimatur on the conservative Serbian program would have been a great boon.

---

80. Vidaković's Foreword was reprinted in Karadžić, *SG*, I, 113–118.

Vidaković gave only a paragraph from Dobrovský's letter. Since the "patriarch of Slavic linguistics" was an extremely cautious man, it is probable that he accompanied the quoted statement with qualifying remarks, which the novelist did not want to include. Dobrovský may have pointed out, as he did elsewhere, that there should be one "middle way," not many, and that Serbia still lacked a linguist to lay the ground rules for the kind of selection he envisaged. Vidaković himself had indicated in his "Observation" that there was no single, generally-accepted Serbian authority, and he had called for a meeting of learned men to lay the foundation for a formalized literary language. Yet in *Ljubomir, Part II*, he left to individual "taste (vkus)" the charting of a "middle way." Vidaković's words themselves betray the fact that his preference had turned toward what Kopitar called *macaronismus*, the heavily-mixed language he had recently renounced: "Sloga moego i ezyka što se kasa, to napredъ Vamъ dobrii čitateli kažemъ, da samь ja i u ovoj časti, više zarъ neželi i u pervoj, Slavenskago našego ezyka okončenija uzymao, i komu se godь ovo ne dopada, ja molimъ, neka mi oprosti, ja imamъ ovakovyj vkusъ (*SG*, I, 113). Nothing favorable can be said for the arbitrary, functionless mixing of Russian and Serbian words and desinences in this quotation. Dobrovský may well have supported the novelist in theory, but he could hardly have countenanced his new practices. The excessive intercalation of Russian Slavonic seemed to reflect defiance rather than strong conviction. The cause of effecting a suitable and speedy solution to the Serbian language problem was not served by Vidaković's petulant reaction to Vuk's misdirected criticism.

With respect to alphabet and orthography, Vidaković had always been ultraconservative; he had even criticized Dositej Obradović for his "poor" orthography. In *Ljubomir, Part I*, he had presented the unusual combination of a reasonably contemporary language in a completely archaic dress, with symbols and orthography of the fashion suggested by Mrazović. By the time he wrote *Part II* of his novel, the writer knew that Karadžić was the anonymous assailant of *Usamljeni Junoša*; he had also seen the unfriendly reception given the *Pismenica* in the Vojvodina. In his Foreword, Vidaković hastened to attack Vuk's book at the point he considered most sensitive and controversial:

And I will confess the truth to you my readers, that I cannot stop wondering at that writer and how he dared venture to pierce our alphabet to its vital nerve, and to leave out such a great number of our most beautiful letters, about sixteen, without which we cannot be!

Let us protect our letters, my beloved readers, and let us preserve them as our priceless wealth, and as our one most beautiful treasure (*SG*, I, 113–114).

Vidaković's defense of the inviolability of the Serbian Slavonic letters (all forty-two of them, including such anachronisms as ы, ъ, ѕ, and ѭ) guaranteed him the unrestrained applause of the Orthodox Church, which had long regarded its obscurantist alphabet as a repository for the precious icons of national cultural identity. Fifty years earlier the Vojvodina hierarchy had bitterly and successfully fought against the Vienna-proposed use of Latin letters in Serbian secular books printed by Kurzbeck. Indeed, in 1817, the same year as the publication of *Ljubomir, Part II*, the church had persuaded Sava Mrkalj, author of the progressive "Fat of the Thick Jer," to publish an article in *Novine Serbske*, reversing his previous stand and staunchly defending the use of that letter.[81] But Vidaković's retention of the full alphabet was another tactical error in his battle with Vuk, and a step backward, since several Serbs had already used a simplified orthography in their writing. His orthography was so reactionary and anti-Dositejist that it appeared ludicrous even to those who otherwise sympathized with him during his troubles with Karadžić and Kopitar.

The Vienna pair might have overlooked Vidaković's quarrelsome, but largely ineffective remarks, had the novelist not brought "the second Cyril" into the quarrel. Kopitar had maintained a deeply personal as well as scholarly relationship with Dobrovský since 1808. Never noted for magnanimity in debate, the Slovene was driven to fury by Vidaković's "abuse of your authority," as he wrote to Dobrovský. He also realized that Vidaković's one-paragraph citation from the Czech's letter gave the impression of full support for his "middle way" (or ways). If it should appear that Dobrovský favored the Slaveno-Serbs, Vuk's reforms would suffer a further loss of prestige in Serbia. This combination of emotional and tactical con-

81. Reprinted in Karadžić, *SG*, I, 219–220.

siderations accounts for the ruthless thoroughness with which Vuk and Kopitar prepared their critique of *Ljubomir*, *Parts I* and *II*.

Kopitar's correspondence with Dobrovský during the summer of 1817 shows his restless attempts to commit the Czech to their side in the controversy, but the wise abbot tactfully refused: "I can well beware of taking sides in this. Unfortunately!" (*BDK*, p. 432). In July, Kopitar wrote to Dobrovský, in Latin, informing him of the publication of *Part II* of *Ljubomir* and the inclusion in its Foreword of the quote from Dobrovský's letter. Kopitar told his mentor that he and Vuk were writing a review that he hoped would put an end to this and similar quarrels, especially among the Greeks and Serbs.[82] He also included a list of questions on the Serbian language from Vuk.

Dobrovský's answer was a clear exposition of his attitude toward the incipient Serbian language struggle. He evidently had not given Vidaković permission to quote his letter, for he expressed surprise at being involved in the current debate: "What is this about a middle style that the Serbs are supposed to adopt?" Besides answering Vuk's questions, he outlined here and there what he thought the Serbian literary language should and should not include. He opposed orthographical inconsistency: "If anyone writes мѣcѣцъ, мѣcѧцъ, мѣcѣцъ, меcецъ, his orthography is inconsistent, and this I do not approve of" (*BDK*, p. 427). Dobrovský also disapproved the alternation of Slavonic and vernacular desinences for the same grammatical form: "He who prefers *momaka* to *momkov* (genitive plural) ought to do so always. One ought not to deal completely arbitrarily with the endings -*ami* and -*ama* [the Russian and Serbian instrumental plurals], although some freedom should be allowed to poets." The samples of language submitted by Karadžić had been taken from Vidaković's *Ljubomir*, and were intended to display the novelist's orthographical and morphological vacillation and thus prove to Dobrovský that the novelist's "middle way" was no way at all.

Although he had no respect for Vidaković's linguistic waywardness, Dobrovský's corrective eye penetrated more deeply and fretfully into Vuk's own vernacular-structured language. Like

82. "Finem imponet, spero, liti inauditae inter ceteras nationes, praeter Graecos et Serbos," Dobrovský, *BDK*, p. 425. The affection of the two men for one another appears in the salutations to their letters. Dobrovský often called Kopitar "Slavin" and "lieber Slavin," while his disciple called him "Meister" and "Verehrtester Meister."

Vidaković, Dobrovský believed that "corruptions" or "poor pronunciation" in everyday speech (*krv, dug*) should be "corrected" in writing, in terms of Slavonic. In his letter the Czech linguist included as "corruptions" some of today's standard literary forms, such as *sunce, vuk* (his questioner's first name), *suza*, and *vidio*. He preferred to have them written *slnce, vlk, slza*, and *vidil*, remarking that the only form Vidaković would not accept was *vidil* (*BDK*, p. 429). But when it came to restoring the "poorly pronounced" forms, Dobrovský had an advantage over other linguists, in that he possessed a solid conception of the language of the early Slavonic writings. He could distinguish between "pure Slavonic" and native Russian forms, a talent generally lost to Slavdom since Smotrick time. Because he had been working for years on an Old Slavonic grammar, Dobrovský could write: "слънце, длъгъ, and пръстъ without the vowel are pure Slavonic, and the insertion of the vowel in *solnce, dolg, perst* is new" (*BDK*, p. 427). This particular quotation highlights the principal theoretical problem faced by the Slaveno-Serbs, for what Dobrovský called "new" were precisely the Russian Slavonic words that Vidaković was bent on restoring, thinking them ancient Serbian.

An important Karadžić innovation that Dobrovský could not accept was the use of the general case endings *-ima* and *-ama* for the locative plural: "Thus, also у печатным книгама (in my eyes) is wrong." Dobrovský wanted to restore the *h* ending to the locative plural, even though he mistakenly believed that this phoneme no longer existed in spoken Serbian; in this assumption he was depending on Vuk's information, which at that time was still incomplete. Dobrovský's retort to Vuk's contention that pure Serbian had never been published in Cyrillic letters revealed his irritation with the Vienna pair's insistence on a literary language based entirely on the vernacular: "I am not wholly of Vuk's opinion. If pure Serbian has not yet been printed in Cyrillic books, then I can say to you that true Czech (the new, common speech) has still not been written in any book. There is a mixture, but no style has yet been new, unmixed" (*BDK*, p. 429). Dobrovský, like the Slaveno-Serbs, favored synthetic languages, created from a mixture of the vernacular and the ancient Slavonic. His friendship for Kopitar probably kept him from becoming a more active ally on the side of the Vojvodina group.

Although in his letter he continually returned to his cherished idea of the middle style, he never legislated but merely offered his preferences:

> But I would wish that on certain points, which certainly must be more closely defined, one would abandon the completely vulgar new pronunciation and maintain the older, more correct Slavonic. And one may well call this the middle style ... I believe that if one omits the Turkish (foreign) words of the vulgar language and sets in their place the pure Slavonic (Old Serbian), if one avoids certain corruptions (bad pronunciations) and restores the more correct, such a selection in orthography can be called the middle style (e veteri et nova lingua compositus) (*BDK*, pp. 427–428).

From his detached vantage-ground, the Prague Slavist could observe that one vital element was missing to ensure the success of his middle style in the Vojvodina, and he admitted this failing to Kopitar, the chief opponent of his plan: "But who will set up the principles by which the selection of the old and the usable new could be tested? Without such principles, which Serbs who write must adhere to, an adequate language can never be hoped for in their writings" (*BDK*, p. 428).

Dobrovský understood and tolerated Kopitar's vengeful personality. Indeed, in view of the many violent quarrels engaged in by the Slovene censor, he seems to have been compelled always to prove himself right; in his mind, anyone who disagreed with him (except Dobrovský) was persecuting him. Kopitar's very first letter to Dobrovský, in April 1808, while paying tribute to Dobrovský's journal *Slavin*, did not neglect the opportunity to complain that Valentin Vodnik had been trying to prevent publication of his *Grammatik*, and he belittled Vodnik in his characteristically nasty way (*BDK*, p. 1). Dobrovský's awareness of Kopitar's proclivity for abuse, as well as genuine sympathy for Vidaković, may explain his concern over the revenge being prepared by the Slovene and his disciple: "Likely the 'Critique' on Vidaković will prove better than the old remarks on his style ... One should not pounce on him so because of his mixed style. He was able, nevertheless, to take pains" (*BDK*, p. 432).

"The Second Serbian Critique," as the review of *Parts I* and *II* of *Ljubomir* was entitled, is commonly ascribed to Vuk Karadžić. It would be more realistic, and more complimentary to Vuk's memory, to view this fifty-page work as a collaboration with Kopitar, for it was not just a review but an assassination. The first thirty-two pages were devoted to an analysis of the plot, interwoven with the kind of running diatribe and nasty digressions in which Kopitar had long experience. His hand was visible at the very beginning, where he remarked of Ljubomir's method of teaching children: "From this it is evident that Ljubomir read Rousseau, but it is a shame that he did not have the brains to figure out that Rousseau was right in many things, but here and there he was crazy, just like him, only more intelligently" (*SG*, I, 118–119). The literary part of the review combined Kopitar's well-informed sarcasm with Vuk's vernacular authenticity and *prosto* vulgarity. Of a Vidaković description of a young girl's shyness, Vuk commented: "This is somewhat similar to a shy little whore." The summation of this long, tireless dismemberment of the structure of Vidaković's novel gives a sufficient picture of Kopitar's rage:

> In his reply to the first critique Mr. V. asked which novels were to the reviewer's taste. Now it is not necessary to tell him to read Wieland's *Agathon, Amadis, Oberon, Aristippus, The Golden Mirror, The Abderites,* and the rest; Goethe's *Wilhelm and Werther;* Fénelon's *Télémaque*... Lesage's *Gil Blas* and *Le Diable boiteux;* Goldsmith's *Vicar of Wakefield;* Richardson's *Clarissa;* Fielding's *Tom Jones;* Sterne's *Shandy,* and other novels similar to these. But let him take the worst German novel, which even the maids don't read, and he will see that it is more intelligently written than his *Ljubomir.* In the novels cited man is presented *as he is* and *how he ought to be.* There an intelligent and respectable man speaks and acts everywhere as intelligent and respectable; a fool like a fool; a bad and worthless man like a bad and worthless man; a whore like a whore, etc. But here in some places Ljubomir and Svetozar speak and act like clowns and bad people; Draginja and Melissa like whores; and Vlajko and Agapija moralize like Socrates.
>
> From all this, we must conclude that Mr. V. knows neither *history,* nor *geography,* nor *logic,* nor *poetry,* nor *rhetoric;* nor does he know what *morality* is, nor *shame,* nor *politeness;* nor does he know the *character of our people,* or *anything* (*SG*, I, 146–147).

What Kopitar did to the content, Karadžić did to the language. The linguistic analysis was not half so long as the literary critique,

3—H.S.S.

but it managed to complete the job of destroying Vidaković's reputation as a writer. Vuk took advantage of the fact that Vidaković had left himself vulnerable by renouncing in *Part II* the linguistic views set forth in his Introduction to *Part I*: "Even though Mr. Author set certain rules on language in the first part, his second part is much worse and more abominable." Karadžić did not bother, however, to test the language in *Part I* against the principles in the "Observation"; rather, he lumped the two parts together and treated his samples as though they all came from the same font. His criticisms fell within the same general areas outlined in his first critique: use of Slavonic vocabulary instead of Serbian, use of Slavonic morphology, incorrect Serbian syntax, orthographical inconsistency, and use of Vojvodina dialect forms.

Vidaković's language in *Part I* was reasonably consistent (as is shown in my Appendix). It appears, therefore, that Vuk either took most of his examples from *Part II* or searched widely through both parts in order to present an unflattering picture. As a matter of fact, *Part I* was fully understandable for the general reader, as the author contended. A close linguistic analysis would have been ineffective, forcing Vuk to furnish "spoken" equivalents for Vidaković's Russian Slavonisms when indeed no such lexical items existed. Vuk would have been confronted by the same problems of vocabulary that the Vojvodina Serbs had been contending with for the three decades since Dositej had exhorted them to write for the people. But Vuk made no attempt to put himself into Vidaković's shoes and thus protected himself from the inevitable criticism.

It was against Vidaković's (and Dobrovský's) contention that the Serbian literary language should undergo a transfusion from Russian Slavonic that Vuk struck his heaviest blow. For purposes of analogy, he turned to the German literary language, which he stated had been based for over three hundred years on the Saxon dialect and not on "corrected" Austrian. Next he used a rhetorical device which, by its erudition and subtlety, could only be Kopitar's invention. After giving examples of the Lord's Prayer from four different periods of German literature, he proceeded to build two new versions, based on a mixture of the language from all four periods. He called the new mixture "Goto-Nemački" (Gotho-German), to parallel Slaveno-Serbian. The four historical examples were:

I. *Оче нашъ Вулфилинъ лѣта 375.*

Atta unsar, Θu in himinam,
Weihnai namo Θein,
Quimai Θiudinassus Θeins,
Wairθai wilja Θeins, swe in himina, jah ana airθai.
Hlaif unsarana Θana sinteinan gif uns himmadaga,
Jah aflet uns Θatei skulans sijaima, swaswe jah weis afletam
    Θaim skulam unsaraim,
Jah ni bringais uns in fraistubnjai,
Ak lausei uns af Θamma ubilin.

II. *Оче нашъ калугьера на Райни лѣта 850.*

Fater unser, Θu in himilon pist,
Giwihit si namo Θin,
Quaeme richi Θin,
Werdhe willeo Θin, sama so in himile, endi in erθu.
Broot unseraz emezzigan gib uns hiutu,
Endi ferlaz uns sculdhi unsero, samo so wir farlazzan
    scolom unserem,
endi ni giledi unsih in Costunga,
auh arlosi unsih fona Ubile.

III. *Оче нашъ у другога калугьера лѣта 890.*

Fater unser, thu thar bist in himile,
si geheilagot thin namo,
Queme thin rihhi (— рихи —),
si thin willo, so her in himilo ist, so si her in erdu.
Unsar Brot tagalihhaz gib uns hiutu,
inti furlaz uns unsera sculdi, so wir furlazemes unsaron
    sculdigon,
inti ni geleitest unsih in kostunga,
Uz ouch arlosi unsih fon Ubile.

IV. *Оче нашъ данашньій лѣта 1817.*

Vater unser, der du bist in dem Himmel,
Geheiliget werde dein Nahme,
Dein Reich komme,
Dein Wille geschehe, wie im Himmel so auch auf Erden.
Unser täglich Brot gib uns heute,
Und vergib uns unsere Schuld, wie wir vergeben unsern
    Schuldigern,
Und führe uns nicht in Versuchung,
Sondern erlöse uns von dem Uebel.

The two new "Slaveno-Serbian" (or "Gotho-German") versions proposed by Vuk were:

> Atta unsar thu in himilon pist,
> Gewihit si thin namo,
> Queme Reich thin,
> Werdhe wilja thin, swe in himina, endi in erthu.
> Hlaif unsaran tagalihhan gib uns hiutu,
> Endi farlazz uns unsera skuldi, swe jah weis forlazzan
>   unsaron skuldigon,
> Endi ni giledi unsih in costunga,
> Ouch arlosi uns af ɵamma ubilin.

> Fater unsar, der ɵu pist in dem himinam,
> Geheiligot werde namo Ɵein,
> Dein Ɵiudinassus quaeme,
> Thin Wille wairɵai, so im himile, jah auf erɵu.
> Unseraz Brot sinteinan gif uns himmadaga,
> Und aflet uns unsera Schuld, so wie vergeben unsaraim
>   scolon,
> Endi füre uns ni in Versuchung,
> Ak erlöse uns fona Ubile.

(SG, I, 158–159)

According to Karadžić, these samples illustrated "the way Mr. V. and some of our other writers build the literary language. Mr. Vidaković's style is even funnier and much worse than these Gotho-German *Our Fathers*."

To equate Slaveno-Serbian with a fictitious Gotho-German language was a brilliant stroke, whose sardonic humor might have amused even Vidaković's strongest sympathizers. But was it an appropriate comparison? Did Russian Slavonic and spoken Serbian differ nearly as much as fourth-century Gothic and the literary German of 1817? A juxtaposition of the Russian Slavonic Lord's Prayer with the version in Vuk's translation of the *New Testament* shows that the differences were insignificant by comparison with the differences between the Gothic and German versions. His method of ridicule was really a reduction by absurdity, not to absurdity.

The use of the Lord's Prayer further implicates Kopitar in the preparation of the review. Adelung, whom Kopitar so greatly admired, had collected some 500 versions, "for indeed it is the only formula one can have in so many languages, and . . . it has great advantages also with regard to correctness."[83] In the second volume of *Mithridates*, published after Adelung's death, appeared the three archaic versions of the prayer given by Vuk—a striking coincidence indeed! The Vuk texts differed from those in *Mithridates*, only in three minor spelling points, although Vuk did omit the final line from the Gothic. The suspicion that this was Kopitar's clever device is supported by a letter from him to Karl Rumy, Director of the Karlovci Gymnasium, a few months before the review was published: "Is not this Slaveno-Serbian *macaronism*," he exclaims, "just as though I were to take Ulfila's or even Ottfried's language and grammar and yoke them together with Luther and Goethe!"[84]

Throughout their review of *Ljubomir*, Vuk and Kopitar seemed obsessed with the fear that Dobrovský might again speak on Vidaković's behalf. Thus, they tried to demonstrate that the novelist's language was far from satisfying the requirements of the Czech scholar's middle style. Kopitar's correspondence with Dobrovský was useful in providing guidelines for their criticism. The language samples submitted earlier by Vuk for Dobrovský's commentary were from *Ljubomir*, and those examples which the scholar deemed unacceptable were used in the review. In this way the Vienna pair tried to obviate any possibility of Dobrovský's supporting Vidaković. Nor were they satisfied with having neutralized Dobrovský, for they tried to demonstrate that he was, more or less, on their side: "Dobrovský is only half against us, but completely against him." They naively asked whether there was any more beautiful example of Dobrovský's middle style than the language of the Serbian peasant—which suggestion was an outrageous distortion of the great scholar's position.

Vuk's pursuit of Vidaković did not end with this review. In 1817 and 1819 the novelist published notices of advanced subscription for a Part III of *Ljubomir*. Karadžić reacted to each of these announcements with brief articles in the *Novine Serbske*, taunting Vidaković for his subscription troubles and suggesting that it was his failure to answer Vuk's criticism that was responsible for his present problems. Indeed, the Vuk–Kopitar review, which had appeared twice a week for six weeks in *Novine Serbske*, had made a laughing stock of "the

83. J. C. Adelung, *Mithridates*, I, p. xvi.
84. Kopitar, *Kopitars Briefwechsel mit Karl Georg Rumy*, p. 20.

Serbian Walter Scott," as his admirers called him. Part III of *Ljubomir* was finally published in 1823. There was a note of tired desperation in its Introduction, as Vidaković wrote concerning his assailant: "Only let him show me in a decent manner, and not as my critic, who raises his voice like some dictator." The review had in fact been thoroughly dogmatic and frequently ruthless, and was not at all conducive to the reasonable exchange of ideas on a new literary language that both Vidaković and Vuk had sought in 1814.

CONCLUSION

This investigation into the origins of the Serbian language controversy in the nineteenth century was prompted by a conjecture that the invariably idealized accounts of Vuk Karadžić's role have fostered misconceptions about the basic issues involved. The study reveals that the novelist Milovan Vidaković was the representative of a native intellectual movement, stemming from Dositej Obradović and related in its linguistic theory to the philosophy of Josef Dobrovský, the outstanding Slavic philologist of his day. The early language program of Vuk was in fact alien in origin, developed and promoted from outside the Serbian cultural milieu. The nub of the quarrel between him and Jernej Kopitar, on one side, and the Slaveno-Serbs, on the other, lay in Kopitar's minimization of dialect differences and his oversimplification of Adelung's theory of orthography.

The Vojvodina was the core of Serbian intellectual life in the early nineteenth century, and it was there that the new literary language should have evolved. Vidaković's "Observation on the Serbian Language" demonstrated that this writer was consciously working toward a vernacular-based idiom. An analysis of the language in *Ljubomir, Part I* (see Appendix) shows that it was essentially spoken Serbian with Vojvodina dialectisms. Vidaković's language proposals in the "Observation" were not so different from those made by Vuk Karadžić shortly afterward, but Vuk's subsequent attack on an early novel drove the writer into the waiting arms of the church. It was the emotional factor, not theoretical differences, that turned the debate into a "war."

It seems indisputable that the Serbs would have developed a suitable literary language without the aid of the Slovene Kopitar. The theories of Adelung and Humboldt notwithstanding, literary languages develop in an organic process, which seldom coincides with that of the spoken language. Although the Serbian literary and vernacular idioms were quite distinct, by the crucial year 1814 they were beginning to converge, and their fusion seemed inevitable to all who were not blinded by religio-linguistic fantasies. Men like Vidaković tried to accelerate the process. They were inconsistent, and they made mistakes that were apparent to many, but in time the literary language would have become normalized and the Russian Slavonic elements would have been assimilated or eliminated by the Serbian, as Vidaković himself predicted. The Slaveno-Serbian language movement was alive and growing when Kopitar and Vuk made their attack on Vidaković. In the beginning it was the acerbic personality of Kopitar that inflamed the quarrel, but subsequently the deep emotional and psychic elements inherent in language helped to stoke the fires of controversy. The unwillingness of Vidaković and the Slaveno-Serbs to accept Vuk's backwoods vernacular had a practical as well as aesthetic justification, for they correctly felt that at this culturally-anemic stage the Serbian language needed a lexical transfusion. The controversy between Vuk and the Vojvodina lasted nearly fifty years; it was won by the Karadžić forces at great cost to the energies and direction of the national revival.

I hope that I have shown that Vuk and Kopitar were at least as responsible for the beginning of the War for a Serbian Language and Orthography as were the Slaveno-Serbs. I also trust that someday the early cultural achievements of the Vojvodina Serbs will be re-examined in a fresh light, and that men like Milovan Vidaković will be given the credit they deserve for their contribution to the Serbian Renaissance.

APPENDIX

The Language in Vidaković's *Ljubomir u Elisiumu, Part I*

On opening to the title page of *Ljubomir u Elisiumu, Part I*, the reader receives the impression that this is a Russian book of the 1790's. One meets such phrases as: "моралная повѣсть, сочинена... дѣтовоспитателемъ; посвящена же... младому купцу и гражданину; въ Будимѣ." Yet there are native Serbian elements as well—for example, у Елісіуму (not въ Елісіумѣ), and the first epithet describing the *povѣstь* is романтическа (not -ая), while the dedication is господару (not -рю). The title page can be said to be in high-style Russian, with a few Serbianisms.

The opening of the flowery dedication to the patron who financed the publication continues in the same style: "Древо се на древо, вели наша Сербска пословица, осланя, а человѣкъ на человѣка" (A tree leans on a tree, says our Serbian proverb, and a man on a man)." This saying in Vuk's collection of proverbs reads, "*Drvo se na drvo naslanja a čoek na čoeka*" (modern standard would have "*čovek na čoveka*"). The percentage of Russian Slavonicisms decreases, but remains relatively high throughout the short dedication and the dozen pages of the address to "My Dearest Readers." The eighteen pages of the "Примѣчаніе о Сербскому езыку" is much less Slavonic, although its section on the history of the Slavs reverts to an elevated style that again approximates contemporary Slavonic-tinged Russian. Yet in this "Observation on the Serbian Language" Vidaković expressly rejects the idea of writing either Slavonic or its opposite, the language of the *baba* in the kitchen. He is setting out to write "правый нашъ Сербскій езыкъ."

To measure his success, I examined the approximately six hundred pages of *Ljubomir, Part I*, comparing Vidaković's language with today's literary *štokavian*. Any element that deviates from the twentieth century standard was classified as deriving from Russian Slavonic, from the general Vojvodina dialect or one of its subdialects, or simply as anomalous. Of course, I should point out that Vidaković's Slavonic orthography inhibits a totally accurate description of his language. Although he shuns a few of the more esoteric letters recommended by Mrazović's *Rukovodstvo*, his spelling generally follows the rules given in that book. The results of my analysis of the language of *Ljubomir, Part I*, are herewith condensed in an eclectic survey, combining remarks on phonology, morphology, and orthography with references to historical linguistics where needed.

In Serbian one expects the vowel *a* where Common Slavic had the old jers, ь or ъ in strong position; in Russian Slavonic, one expects *e* or *o*, respectively. Russian-Slavonic Church pronunciation led to *e* and *o* in the spelling of various words with a jer historically in weak position. Vidaković uses a liberal sprinkling of words with the *e/o* reflexes, for like Dositej he ordinarily borrows Russian Slavonic words without Serbianizing them. Some typical Slavonicisms of this sort are *sočiniteľ*, *sotvorihъ*, *soveršeno*, *so timъ* (thereby), *ljubovъ*, *čestъ*, *voistinu*, *vooruža*, *voshititelnoj*, *ostatokъ* and *doždъ*. Although the productive prefix *uz-* (from **vъz-*) is common in his writing, Vidaković still Slavonicizes it to make *vozbuntuje* with a Germanic, though well-domesticated, root. On the whole, he uses the ordinary Serbian, as in *otacъ*, *sladakъ*, *silanъ*, *danъ*, and the like. With the past participles of *ići* compounds he always uses the native *pošao*, *došao*, etc.—a form that Dobrovský did not approve.

In Vidaković's usage the "thick jer" *ъ* must be written at the end of any word that does not already end in a vowel letter. The "thin yer" also occurs in final position, where it sometimes is justifiable in terms of etymology (*danь*) or morphophonemics (*radostь*), it sometimes represents the weight of Russian Slavonic tradition (*vidišь*, *znašь*), but it often merely serves as a diacritic showing that the preceding consonant letter denotes a palatal consonant.

There is a series of orthographic problems, connected on the one hand with the Slavonic letters (chiefly *ы*, *u*, *ï*, *ŭ*, *v*, *ѣ*), and on the other, with the Serbian sounds: reflexes of **i*, **y*, and **ě* and the Serbian palatals *ć*, *đ*, *lj*, *nj*, and *j*. For example, Vidaković uses all four of the Slavonic symbols that a Serb would pronounce *i*, which are given by Mrazović as *u*, *ы*, *ï*, and *v*, and he is moderately consistent in following the rules:

(1) The *ï* appears before vowels and in foreign words: *примѣчанïе*, *возсïяти*, *нïе*, *медïцïна*. (*Вïно* is apparently regarded as foreign.)

(2) Of *u* and *ы* (regarded as alternate forms by Mrazović, pp. 20–21), *u* is to be written "at the beginning of Slavic words," at the end of participles and adjectives "when it is preceded by *ï* or *ы*" (*that is, for* Nominative singular masculine), after *g*, *k*, and *h* if not followed by a vowel, and "in all Slavonic expressions where one does not have to put *ï* or *ы*." Mrazović states that *ы* should be written in the "final syllable of participles and adjectives of singular number when it is followed by *ŭ*"; after *ц*; "at the end of adverbs ending in *-жды*"; and "at the end of some nominal, pronominal and participial cases," which are to be learned later in the grammar. Finally, Mrazović gives long lists of words that use *ы* internally, as well as those that have the soft masculine singular nominative adjectival ending *ïŭ*.

Mrazović provides no specific guide for the use of *ŭ* versus *u*, but it is clear from his total usage that *ŭ* is to be written after vowels. In rare instances this symbol, which can usually be read *j*, really represents *i*: *отъ нïŭ* = *ot nji(h)*.

(3) The *v*, to be used "in some foreign words," does appear in a very few Vidaković borrowings, ultimately of Greek origin, such as *гѵмназïя*, *лѵра*..

Vidaković expressly intended to write ѣ in its proper etymological place, "even though we in Srem always say *e*." He evidently attributed to the letter the pronunciation described by Mrazović (p. 20) as "iděže slivaemoe ĭe slyšitsja"—which surely means *je*. Vidaković manages very nicely with roots and Slavonic borrowings (*vněšnja*, etc.), but dialect pronunciations cause difficulty in the common adverbs of place: *gdi*, *gdě*, *gdĭe*; *nigdě*, *nigdi*. With rare roots (*izlema*) he tends to write simply the *e* of his own pronunciation. In nonpresent forms of old *ě*-verbs he regularly uses *i*, in accord with his own Vojvodina dialect:[85] *želili*, *želiti*, *viditi*, *vidila*.

Vuk's greatest orthographical achievement was the unambiguous representation of *j* and the palatals *nj*, *lj*, *ć*, and *đ* (*j њ љ ħ ђ*). Vidaković and other Serbs of the day, including Vuk in his early writings, found it very hard to be consistent with the multiplicity of devices used to represent these sounds. Yod in initial or postvocalic position was spelled in a variety of ways. Vidaković regularly uses *ї* in the few cases where *o* follows (*моїой*, *їоцъ*) and in the exclamation *ïao* (but also *яо*). Otherwise, for yod before *a* and *u*, the letters *я* and *ю* serve (*моя*, *мою*), although *їa* for *ija* does occur (according to a Slavonic tradition not consistently followed by Mrazović), as in *провїнцїа*. The letter *e* does double duty, to represent *e* (rarely, as in *ето*, *ево*) and *je* (usually as in *e*, *еданъ*, *мое*). Before *i*, there is no indication at all: *мои* = *moji*, and yod final is written *й*, e.g., *мой*.

The palatal quality of *lj* and *nj* is indicated by *ь* (*конь*, *смиль*, *ньїове* = *konj*, *smilj*, *nji[h]ove*), by *я* and *ю* (*коня*, *землю*), by *њ* (*конѣ*, *землѣ*), or occasionally not at all, especially before *i* (*читатели*), or inconsistently (*нїови кони пуштени* = *njihovi konji pušteni*, *нїомъ* = *njom*). Vidaković often spells common words having these sounds in more than one way (*болье*, *болѣ*). Vidaković follows a well-established tradition in writing *тъ* for the voiceless palatal *ć* (*ħ*): *ретьитье*, *нетьу*. Indeed, he uses *ħ* once: *Младиħъ* (p. 414). With some Russian-Slavonic borrowings he retains the Slavonic letter *щ*, originally stemming from the Bulgarian *št* < **tj*: *просвѣщенъ*, *просвѣщенїе*, *священъ*, *восхищенъ*. In some words Vidaković alternately writes *шт* and *щ*.

With the voiced counterpart *đ* (*ђ*), however, Vidaković seems slightly more reluctant about reflecting the native pronunciation. When he does,

85. Pavle Ivić, *Die serbokroatischen Dialekte*, I, 172. Aside from Ivić's information about the dialects of the Vojvodina, the most useful source has been Berislav Nikolić's monograph on the Srem dialect, *Sremski govor*, although helpful details may be gleaned from other works cited in the bibliography.

Just as this essay was going to press, I was able to look through Jovan Kašić, *Jezik Milovana Vidakovića* (Novi Sad: Filozofski fakultet, 1968). It is a detailed study of the language of Vidaković's *Autobiography* (posthumous, 1871), with valuable comparisons to the usage of older and contemporary Vojvodina writers. Kašić points out that Vidaković writes in popular language, but he does not treat the differences between the style and language of the *Autobiography* and other works, and he barely mentions the controversy with Vuk.

he writes *dъ*, like the early Vuk and others before him: *сладье, младьа*, and the like. A few examples with *я* and *ю* occur, such as *дяволъ, сѣдяше* (3rd singular imperfect). Vidaković prefers the Slavonic *žd* (ultimately of Bulgarian origin, but favored by Russians, especially for high style) in a series of individual words and in past passive participles and verbal substantives. Thus, he writes *prežde, meždu* (and its Slavonicized Serbian mate *izmeždu*), *-hožda-, graždaninъ*, and forms like *roždenъ, uslaždenie, uvreždenъ* and *pobuždenie*. Even such a typically Serbian syntagma as *otъ moe roždene sestre děte* (my sister's child) maintains the Russian Slavonic *žd*. From Russian Slavonic Vidaković (and Mrazović) take the stems *čuž-* (Serbian *tuđ*) and *gospoža*, with the Russian *ž* that had replaced the expected Bulgarian *žd*.

Vidaković maintains that rapid speech includes some automatic changes that must not be written, for they do not correspond to the essence of the language (*svojstvo jezika*). "Even though in rapid pronunciation we say *trkъ, krvъ, grkъ, trnъ, drvo, grmъ*, etc., we must write *terkъ, krovъ, grekъ, ternъ, drevo, gremъ*." Clearly enough, his guide is Russian Slavonic, for where else could he learn whether to write the vowel before or after *r*? But Russian Slavonic is not a reliable guide, as is shown by the last word, which is scarcely to be found in the ordinary church texts, much less in Russian books. The general rule is of course: "write *er* for syllabic *r*, except for specific words like *krv, grk*, and *drvo*." Vidaković follows it well, even where Russian Slavonic has *or* (*kerčma, tergovacъ*), but with occasional vernacular-oriented lapses (*grlo* a few times beside the usual *gerlo*, zagerli; *u pomrčini* beside *pomerčini*). From the vehemence of his reaction to Vuk's criticism, one wonders whether in careful speech he might not even have pronounced *zaderži, žertvu, cerkve*, and the like. Vidaković shares with the early Vuk and many contemporary and later writers a reluctance to allow the letter *r* to stand between consonants (see Jonke, *Književni jezik*, pp. 81–105).

For the ancient vocalic *l*, which developed to *ol* in Russian and in the corresponding Slavonic, but to *u* in nearly all štokavian dialects, Vidaković tends rather to the Slavonic usage. Thus, he usually writes *solnce, dolgъ, prodolži, dolžnostъ, polkъ, opolčavati, polnyj, ispolnjava, molnija, izъ volkovyhъ nokatahъ*, and the like, but sometimes *sunce, dužnostъ, punъ*, etc. A Slavonic root with Serbian diminutive suffix is *holmitъe* (accusative plural). Some roots seem to occur only in Serbian form, notably the ubiquitous *suza*, but also *obuče, vuna, jabuka, puža, muzle*, and other relatively rare words.

The Common Slavic front nasal vowel gave *e* in Serbian, but *a* (with preceding palatalization) in Russian Slavonic. Vidaković follows his native language faithfully here; the exceptions are mostly in words that have religious or philosophical nuances, such as *изрядне священнике, дивный порядокъ, посвятимъ, повѣсть посвящена, тягота*, but also *Князь Душанъ*.

Most štokavian dialects lack *h* (Ivić, *Die serbo-kroatischen Dialekte*, p. 98). Vidaković, like Vuk in his early writings, does not recognize *h* in many Serbian words: *ajde, odma, u Ervatskoj* (*Hrvatskoj*), *n'iove* (*njihove*), *n'iovъ dialektъ, usudi se na nъi stati, u ony zemlja, snaa, u kuini* (*kuhini*), *uzdane*. Yet he uses it to differentiate the personal pronoun *ih* from the conjunction *i* (and), although *nъi* is ordinarily written without *h*. In similar fashion Vidaković writes *h* with demonstratives in the genitive plural (*onъ e edanъ otъ ovyhъ*) unless the case is identified by a following noun, such as *otъ ovy zemalja*. Often there is fluctuation (*ora, siroma* beside *orahъ, siromahъ*), but on the whole the *h* appears faithfully in roots (*tihъ, strahъ*) and in desinences (*rekohъ*), and particularly in borrowings from Russian Slavonic (*voshišteno, vozduhъ*).

Vuk criticized Vidaković for using such Russian Slavonic forms as *vsěmъ*, from the old root **vъs-* (all). As a matter of fact, this sort of example is rare in *Ljubomir, Part I*, so that one finds *savъ, sve, sa svimъ, svagda*, or *svaki*, with correct Serbian forms, at every step. Certain terms, usually of abstract meaning, are written unchanged in the Russian Slavonic style: *vseobšta polza*.

The noun, adjective, and pronoun forms in *Ljubomir, Part I*, conform on the whole to modern standard Serbian, with exceptions that generally reflect the spoken language of the Vojvodina. It is noteworthy that the grammatical endings Vidaković uses with borrowed Russian words are generally Serbian rather than Russian Slavonic.

In the instrumental singular of the feminine consonantal stems, the standard desinence is *-ju* (plus softening of stem-consonant), with an optional alternative *-i* if the form is preceded by a preposition or modifier that makes the case clear. Vidaković vacillates between two desinences, *-iju* and *-iom*, with no discernible functional difference. The first would appear to be etymologically oriented, with no indication of the characteristic consonant mutation (*bolestiju* vs. *bolešću*). Vidaković's use of the *-om* ending in *Usamljeni Junoša* was scornfully criticized by Karadžić: "This is something entirely new in the Serbian language! Mr. Author probably wanted to force *bolestъ, pametъ* and other nouns of feminine gender to be declined like *rast*" (*SG*, I, 84). Vuk was mistaken about the novelty of the desinence, which is widespread in the dialects and attested from the beginnings of Serbian writing. It had been in common usage among Slavonian writers of the previous century. It is normal in the Vojvodina, but ordinarily is preceded by a softened stem (*bolešćom*; Nikolić, *Sremski govor*, p. 341; Ivić, *Dialekte*, p. 122). Vidaković does not indicate any consonantal mutation, however, and again he is presumably following an essentially etymological type of spelling, common among his predecessors.

In the oblique cases of the plural, Vidaković departs most radically from the spoken forms.

Serbian ordinarily has the genitive plural desinence *-a* for all but consonant-stem nouns, which have *-i*. One may assume that spellings like *pючïй* stand for this single long *-i*, but the Russian Slavonic *pючeй* also occurs. With masculines, Vidaković often uses the Russian Slavonic desinences. Vuk commented disapprovingly on the presence of *-ov* in *Usamljeni Junoša*; in *Ljubomir, Part I*, it occurs particularly often in passages of high emotion or learned content, as in the "Observation on the Serbian Language": *otъ Slavjanovъ, otъ Grekovъ, častь Slavjanovъ, Serbovъ*, and the like. Here such usage may be borrowed directly from Rajić, on whose *Istorija raznyhъ slavenskihъ narodovъ, naipače Bolgarъ, Horvatovъ i Serbovъ* Vidaković depended for the historical information contained in this digression. Yet this *-ov/-ev* occurs throughout the novel, beside the Serbian *-a* (exceptional *-ahъ*). The Russian *-ej* (*roditelej*) is frequent as well.

It is in the dative, locative, and instrumental plurals that Vidaković's substantive morphology deviates most from the present-day literary language, which follows Vuk's proposed single ending for all three cases (*-ima* or *-ama*). Vidaković's treatment of the locative-instrumental plural of masculine and neuter nouns and of the locative plural of feminine nouns reflects the dialects of Srem and Bačka. His treatment of the dative plural of all genders shows an almost complete dependence upon the Russian Slavonic forms; this is his most striking departure from the morphology of his spoken language.

Štokavian tends to unify the dative, locative, and instrumental plural forms with the terminal desinence *-ma*, but some older forms remain in many dialects. In the Vojvodina the instrumental-locative nonfeminine may still be *-i* (beside the newer, and literary, *-ima*), and in the Srem and Bačka areas the feminine locative may have *-a* (from older *-ah*, with normal loss of *h*; Nikolić, *Sremski govor*, p. 340; Ivić, *Dialekte*, p. 173).

Special care was taken in searching for these case forms. It turned out that almost no deviations from the spoken Vojvodina desinences in instrumental and locative nonfeminine occurred. Exceptions were found in the solemn high style of the Introduction: *zovu se Bolgarami, naimenujuse Serbami*; compare the *-ov* of the genitive plural in the same historical context. The spoken variants *očima* and *očicama* are used several times in the novel itself; they correspond to the Slavonic dual. Some typical instrumental and locative examples are: *sъ ljubezni moi učenicy*; *sravnjamo postupke naše sъ postupcy něgovy*; *sъ Grecy ratъ imati*; *sa svoi znakovi*; *u ednu summu sъ gotovi novcy*; *u koly putujutъi*; *u Sremsky Karlovcy*; *u drugi preděli*; *u ovy rečeny preděly*; *u tvoi děly*; *na vrati moe kolibe*.

Vidaković uses two desinences for the locative plural of feminine nouns: the ordinary Bačka-Srem *a* (< *ah*), and the Russian Slavonic *instrumental* ending *-ami*. For example: *u cerkovny kniga*; *u Grečeski provincia*; *u cesarski deržava*; *u ovy Cesarski strana*; *u ony zemlja*; *u cerny halina*; *u knigami* (several times), *u naukami iskusnějša*. What is interesting is that in the examples found of the *a* desinence the noun is accompanied by a modifier. It is as though Vidaković felt that when he used the short *a* form, which is graphically identical with the nominative singular, he needed a preceding plural-appearing modifier to indicate to the reader that a plural was following (*u ony zemlja*). Vidaković's *-ami* for the locative plural of unmodified feminine nouns is too consistent to be ascribed merely to a poor knowledge of Russian Slavonic. It may well be that he was influenced by the fact that in other dialects of štokavian the instrumental and locative are the same (*-ama*), and thus he associated the Slavonic *-ami* with the locative. This *-ami* ending (for locative plural feminine) also appears in the writings of Dositej Obradović.

Vidaković adopts the Russian Slavonic dative plural endings as part of his program for "correcting" Serbian. He is consistent, admitting few exceptions. Typical examples are: *kъ sěvernymъ stranamъ*; *na razsuždenie pametnimъ mužemъ i blagorevnivimъ dušamъ ostavljamъ*; *i mnogimъ ... zemljamъ Gospoža byla*. The phrase *kъ svoima roditelskima persima* may be regarded as a Slavonic dual, while *kъ konьma* possibly betrays Vidaković's own speech. The author's general uncertainty about the plural cases shows, however, in slips like *u serdcamъ našimъ*, *polĭe se suzamъ* (twice, but also *suzami*).

Vidaković's verb forms are essentially pure Serbian, and deviations from the modern standard can be classified as features of his own dialect. In the present tense, the first person singular always ends in *-m* (except *mogu*, *hoću*), the plural in *-mo*. The third person has no *-t*. In the third plural, beside the standard literary forms, there are many odd endings, unacceptable by today's norms. One finds abundant evidence of the Vojvodina generalization of *-u* and *-du*: *molu* (for *mole*), *čuvu* (*čuvaju*), *načinu* (*načine*); *molidu*, *volidu*, and *nosidu*. Vuk, in his review of *Usamljeni Junoša*, objected strongly to such forms: "But to the misfortune of Serbian literacy, this mistake is not only Mr. Vidaković's, but is found in almost all Serbian books, and the Serbs in towns in Hungary talk that way" (*SG*, I, 85). These suffixes have often been discussed, and they clearly represent a certain leveling of the different endings of the several verbal classes. The process is known throughout the Vojvodina, but with considerable local variations. Vidaković's usage is not internally consistent and cannot be tied to any specific local dialect (see Ivić, *Dialekte*, pp. 122–123; Nikolić, *Sremski govor*, pp. 349–350). Yet in this morphological feature he again is attempting to follow the spoken language.

The literary Serbian simple future (*ja ću pitati* or *pitaću*) is used consistently, as in *služitьešь pri stolu* and *sadъ tьemo i my dojti*. Vidaković again seems to etymologize when the enclitic auxiliary follows the verbal stem, for he sometimes spells the desinence *-ti* that drops in pronunciation—*poslatitьedu* (dialect, 3rd plural) but *platitьu*, *dočekatьešь*, *pytatьemose*. In *izititьemo* the *-ti* may perhaps reflect the spoken form *izićićemo*. The *futurum exactum* also occurs where it is expected syntactically: *ako li se svakomu ovo moe dělo kakove važnosti i ne bude vidilo* [sic]. Neither type of future is found in Russian Slavonic.

Vidaković makes free use of both imperfect and aorist, but since the formations generally coincide in Serbian and Slavonic except for phonological differences that affect the entire system, he can be considered to be following his native usage, with an occasional localism (*imadjaše*) or phonetic Slavonicism, like *uhoždaše* (3rd singular imperfect with the *žd* usual in this root).[86] The perfect regularly uses the auxiliary, as in spoken Serbian (*da sam se ja, koliko sam mogao, i gdi e godъ prilika... donela, trudio*) and observes the gender distinctions in the plural (*koe su... ovce muzle*, feminine plural; *koja su... protekla*, neuter plural). In the Introduction, Vidaković expressly defends on euphonic grounds the use of *-o* (not *-lъ*) in the masculine singular, and he follows this usage without exception. Negation is treated as in modern literary Serbian: *nisamъ znao*. Pluperfects, with either the perfect or imperfect of *biti* as auxiliaries, are used where appropriate: *Polъ dne e vetъ zdravo prevalilo bylo*; *štoste i Vy meni cvětъa byli dali*; *danъ jako ugrějao bjaše*.

In the conditional, Vidaković employs only the enclitic *by* plus the past active participle. At first glance this looks like Russian Slavonic, for standard Serbo-Croatian prescribes the unaccented aorist forms of *biti*, which express person and number. Yet the phonetic loss of *h* in the Vojvodina and elsewhere reduced the first person to the same form as the second and third singular and third plural: *bi*. It is common in various dialects that the other two forms (*bismo, biste*) also reduce to *bi* (Ivić, *Dialekte*, p. 122), and today this unchanging particle is used colloquially by people who write the prescribed longer forms. Thus, Vidaković's usage here should be regarded as native, and from his point of view it had the advantage of corresponding to the church language as well.

Certain features of Vidaković's substantive syntax reflect either the broad features of the Vojvodina-Šumadija dialect or, specifically, those of the Vojvodina subdialect. He tends to use a preposition with the instrumental case when it denotes the means by which an action is performed: *rana* (*hrana*) *sъ kojomъ se ona pita*. He sometimes substitutes the instrumental adjectival ending for locative singular: *u ovimъ selu*. This is a characteristic of the Vojvodina-Šumadija dialect.

Vidaković's frequent use of dative of possession probably comes from Russian Slavonic, although in Serbian it is found in the Torlak dialects and in neighboring Macedonian and Serbian ones (see Ivić, *Dialekte*, p. 125).

One striking construction is *za*+infinitive, usually with a final sense: *za motъi* (in order to be able), *za perkositi starcu* (to annoy the old man). Here are two examples that also serve to illustrate the complex word order

---

86. Today the imperfect is obsolete in the Vojvodina, and the aorist is rare. See Ivić, *Dialekte*, p. 173. Vidaković's easy use of the forms may be evidence that they were still current in his day. It would be interesting to have an analysis of *Ljubomir, Part I*, by a native speaker of a dialect in which the aorist and imperfect are in full use.

Vidaković sometimes admitted: *professor navali na nĭj, da idu sъ nimъ staroga Daskala posětiti, budutъi da e sъ puta vetъ byo došao, i… za prosmějatise malo sъ nimъ"*; *"prosti namъ… za ovu šalu, koju smo izъ naše kъ tebi ljubovi za iskusiti plemenityj duxъ tvoj učinili."* This bizarre construction is found occasionally in the writings of other Serbs. For example, Dositej Obradović writes in his "Letter to Haralampije," *"neću ja čekati da produ dve godine za odgovoriti"* (*Dela*, p. 1). One of the sources given by Đura Daničić in his *Istorija oblika srpskoga ili hrvatskoga jezika do svršetka XVII vijeka* (p. IV) is entitled: Đamanić, P.: *Nauk za pisati dobro latinskiema slovima rieči jezika slovinskoga kojiem se Dubrovčani i sva Dalmatia kako vlastitiem svojiem jezikom služi.*

Kopitar had discussed Vidaković's use of this construction with Dobrovský before the review of *Ljubomir*. Asked for an opinion, Dobrovský wrote: "If the common Serb says *da izbegne* and Vidaković writes *za izbetъi*, I am rather for the first than the second, because the latter is modeled after the Italian" (*BDK*, p. 429). It seems strange that Dobrovský should not have attributed such a construction to the influence of the German *um zu*, particularly with Vidaković. In subsequent scholarly literature *za* + infinitive has been widely commented upon, and is generally agreed to have come from a strong foreign influence, Italian upon the coastal dialects, and German in the old Habsburg empire (Ivić, *Dialekte*, p. 126; Rešetar, *Der štokavische Dialekte*, pp. 214–215).

Lexicographers have not excerpted Vidaković's works, although his vocabulary would be worth a full investigation. Even in the single volume of *Ljubomir, Part I*, he treated so many topics that a rich lexicon was essential, and he himself sought variety and used numerous synonyms. One would like to know how many words he shares with his Vojvodina predecessors and contemporaries, how many with Vuk, and how many were neologisms of his own. Here only a few indications of his usage can be given.

Slavonic, he tells the reader of the "Observation on the Serbian Language," is a source from which to draw "lěpy rěčĭj," although one is not to write Slavonic. Vidaković complains that ordinary speech has been marred by German, Hungarian, and Turkish words, but he himself employs common Serbian words that have been assimilated from varied languages: *vatra, livada, drumъ, kesa, marama, dutьanъ, džepъ, štapъ, tutorъ, momakъ, leptirъ*, and so on. A close study surely would reveal a number of local words like *taki* (at once).

In the absence of a full dictionary, it is hard to spot innovations, but Vidaković points out some possible ones by providing a parenthetical gloss: for example, *dvorъ (avlija)*; *tune (badïeva)*, "gratis"; *ulegati (kalamiti)*, "to graft"; *brana (kapija)*, "gate"; *maslinъ (zejtinъ)*, "oil"; *lixva (ïnteresъ)*; *prilika (fïgura)*, "face"; *ponošenïe (sekiraně)*, "teasing"; *uvida (špïonъ)*; *siněmu (plavetnomu)*.

These words often illustrate capricious and injudicious selection on the part of Vidaković. *Tune* is pure Slavonic, and the form *badïeva* has escaped the lexicographers, who do note *badjava* for the more usual *badava*. *Ulegati, maslinъ* (why not the ordinary *maslo?*), *prilika* (face), and *uvida* (spy) are not felicitous neologisms. *Brana* already means "harrow" in virtually all Slavic dialects, and one is puzzled that Vidaković should have picked it to mean "gate," although it has that sense in Slovene dialects and in Czech and Slovak. Nor is it comprehensible why he objected to *plavetni*. It is only clear that he was striving to improve the language by removing obvious barbarisms. There is one clear example of his didactic intent: on introducing the verb *ispisati* ("paint," a meaning not given by Vuk in his dictionary), he glosses only the first time (*ispišemъ—moluemъ*, p. 458) and then uses it repeatedly without again mentioning the German-derived *malovati* (< *malen*).

Vidaković's most vital non-Serbian source is Russian Slavonic, but the reasons for his selections are not always clear. It is quite understandable that he felt it necessary to employ Slavonic terminology in discussing philosophy or science, but in other situations it is difficult to justify his choice of Russian Slavonic when a suitable Serbian word existed. Why, for example, use *dšti* (*dšter-*) and only very rarely *ktъi* (*ktъer-*)? Why prefer *črezъ* and *skvozъ* to the slightly more usual native *krozъ*? A few of the most common Russian Slavonic expressions in the book are: *abie, obače, inogda, xotja, poneže, voistinu, vsue, počti, tokmo, čestnyj, sověstnyj, obštepoleznyj, vseobštij, vtoryj, pečalenъ, blagosověstne duše, polzu imati, čelověkъ, dvorjaninъ, svidětelь, gradonačalnikъ, tysjaštnikъ, voprosъ, objatïe, štastïe, unynïe, sostojanïe, otečestvo, soobštiti, otvěštati*, and *vozopiti*.

There is a tendency for lexical as well as phonetic and morphological Slavonicisms to appear in more solemn passages, as for example in this philosophical digression (p. 35): "Овый Божїй человѣкъ имаютьи доволно у себи вѣжества, и о воспитанїю человѣку едному свой-ственомъ велико искусство, котому еще любезнѣйше цѣлому человѣ-честву сердце, са строгимъ умомъ, и моралнымъ характеромъ; судити е, како е онъ сада ово двое нѣму особито вовѣреныхъ дѣце воспитати могао."

In dialogue, the novelist's language is generally free of Russian Slavonic influence. In the following conversation, for example, Ljubomir and the Unknown Person speak almost pure Serbian, albeit with certain Vojvodina dialectisms (p. 46):

Непозн: Кога їощь имашь ты у Савїни отъ твоихъ?
Любом: Имамъ едногъ нетьака, отъ мое рождене сестре дѣте.
Непозн: Добро, како му се име?
Любом: Косма.
Непозн: Їоштъ болѣ, отъ колико е година?
Любом: Душа е благо, нисамь му бабине чувао.

74   *Thomas Butler*

Непозн: Хмъ, и то бы нуждно было знати.
Любом: То е найлагкше.
Непозн: А како?
Любом: Отити у исто село, пакъ пытати бабе, оне тье ду знати,
  кое су му бабине чувале.

Or consider the remarks of a young woman on the absurd actions of an
elderly suitor, Parmenion (p. 231): "Ономадъ кадъ самь га видила,
нисамь га силе га убиле ни познати могла: обрїяо и браду и бркове,
да се со тимъ то Боже учини младъ, и мени допадне; а не зна, да ми
е гаднїи у очима, него прїе што е быо." If one changes the Slavonic
so timъ to *stim(e)* and revises the spelling and punctuation, this is a vivid
example of colloquial Serbian. Again (p. 239): "На то ето ти имъ
Старца Парменїона у Вертъ! — Яо! Ето ти ми Куге, рекне сирота,
кадъ га види, кой га бѣсъ садъ овамо донесе."
   In the last analysis, it must be said that Vidaković was too inconsistent
in his use of different kinds of vocabulary. While basically writing a lively
and colloquial Serbian, he sometimes produces a patchwork effect by the
incongruous juxtaposition of disparate elements, as, for example, in the
rhetorical question, "Budala i besporjadočnyj čelověkъ što čini?"—which
joins an emotional and colloquial epithet of Turkish origin to a Russian
Slavonic adjective.
   This cursory analysis shows that the strong Slavonic impression created
by the title page and the introductory salutation, appeal, and essay is
largely false. Vidaković wrote his novel essentially in the idiom spoken in
Vojvodina towns at the beginning of the nineteenth century. This significant fact is obscured first and foremost by the orthography, which generally
clung to the church-oriented norms set by Mrazović's *Rukovodstvo*.
Vidaković's use of *jery* and *jat'* made inconsistency inevitable, for there
was nothing in his spoken language to guide him. His retention of the
superfluous ъ linked him with reactionary circles, particularly the church.
He could easily have avoided many of the charges of archaism and inconsistency that were leveled against him if he had only eliminated ы as
the authoritative Obradović had done, thrown out the "thick jer," as
Mrkalj had recommended, and used ѣ only to represent *e* with palatal
quality in the preceding consonant (нѣму for *njemu*), as Vuk had done in
his first writings. When *Ljubomir* is examined with Vuk's simplified and
consistent orthography in mind, Vidaković's spelling seems ludicrous. Yet
this must not conceal the fact that his phonology is unmistakably that of
spoken Serbian.
   The forms, too, are on the whole those of Vidaković's own speech, and
most of the desinences are still in good use in the literary language. Some
of his deviations from today's norm represent features of the Vojvodina
dialect or its subdialects, and thus they cannot be condemned, for at the
time he was writing, no Serbo-Croatian dialect had been accepted as

standard. Indeed, his dialectisms are no more peculiar than some of Vuk's which have not found general acceptance.[87] Vidaković did tamper with some grammatical desinences, notably the masculine genitive plural, the dative plural of all nouns, and the locative plural feminine, apparently in an attempt to "correct" and enrich the language. Here he was operating in harmony with the theories of Josef Dobrovský, the outstanding Slavicist of the period.

Vuk criticized Vidaković not only for his orthography and morphology, but also for his lexical borrowings from Russian Slavonic. Here the novelist was following the example set by Dositej Obradović and others, but unfortunately he lacked a sense of fitness and measure.

87. For a general view of Karadžić's language as compared to the standard Serbo-Croatian of today, see Milka Ivić, "Jedno poređenje vukovog jezika sa današnjim književnim jezikom."

BIBLIOGRAPHY

Adelung, Johann C. *Deutsche Sprachlehre zum Gebrauche der Schulen in den könig. preuss. Länden.* Berlin, 1781.

————. *Grammatisch-kritisches Wörterbuch der hochdeutschen Mundart, mit beständiger Vergleichung der übrigen Mundarten, besonders aber der Oberdeutschen.* 2 vols. Leipzig, 1793–1801.

————. *Mithridates oder allgemeine Sprachenkunde mit dem Vater Unser als Sprachprobe in beinahe fünfhundert Sprachen und Mundarten.* Vol. I, Berlin, 1806. Vol. II, *Fortgesetzt und bearbeitet von Dr. Johann S. Vater,* Berlin, 1809.

————. *Umständliches Lehrgebäude der deutschen Sprache zur Erläuterung der deutschen Sprachlehre für Schulen.* Leipzig, 1782.

————. *Vollständiger Anweisung zur deutschen Orthographie.* Vienna, 1790.

Auty, Robert. "The Formation of the Slovene Literary Language Against the Background of the Slavonic National Revival," *Slavonic and East European Review,* XLI (London, June 1963), 391–402.

Badalić, Josip. *Jugoslavica usque ad annum MDC: Bibliographie der südslawischen Frühdrucks Aureliae Aquensis.* Baden-Baden: Heitz, 1959.

Banašević, Nikola. "Kako je Vuk postao književnik," *Kovčežić: Prilozi i građa o Dositeju i Vuku,* I (Beograd, 1958), 44–55.

Belić, Aleksandar. *Oko našeg književnog jezika: članci, ogledi i popularna predavanja.* Beograd: Kultura, 1951.

Beneš, Brigit. *Wilhelm von Humboldt, Jacob Grimm, August Schleicher: ein Vergleich ihrer Sprachauffassungen.* Winterthur: Keller, 1958.

Brozović, Dalibor. "Vuk i novoštokavska folklorna koine," *Slavia,* XXXIV (Prague, 1965), 1–27.

Daničić, Đura. *Istorija oblika srpskoga ili hrvatskoga jezika do svršetka XVII vijeka.* Beograd, 1874.

————. "Knjiga Konstantina filosofa o pravopisu," in *Starine,* I. *Jugoslavenska akademija znanosti i umjetnosti* (Zagreb, 1869), 1–43.

————. "Rat za srpski jezik i pravopis," in *Sitniji spisi Đ. Daničića. Srpska kraljevska akademija, Posebna izdanja,* LIV (Beograd, 1925), 5–46.

————. "Rukopis Aleksandrov," *Glasnik društva srbske slovesnosti,* IX (Beograd, 1857), 256–267.

Dimitrijević, Stevan. "Odnošaji pećskih patrijaraha s Rusijom u XVII veku," *Glas srpske kraljevske akademije,* LVIII, *drugi razred,* no. 37 (1900), 201–289; LX, *drugi razred,* no. 38 (1901), 153–203.

Dobrovský, Josef. *Briefwechsel zwischen Dobrowsky und Kopitar (1808–1828)*. Ed. Vatroslav Jagić. St. Petersburg and Berlin, 1885.

Domentijan. *Životi Svetoga Save i Svetoga Simeona*, trans. Dr. Lazar Mirković. *Srpska Književna Zadruga*, XLI, bk. 282. Beograd, 1938.

Džonić, Uroš. "Štampa jugoslavenska," *Jugoslavenska enciklopedija: Narodna enciklopedija srpsko-hrvatsko-slovenačka*, Vol. IV. Ed. Stanoje Stanojević. Zagreb, 1925–1929. Pp. 718–722.

Ferguson, Charles. "Diglossia," *Word*, XV, no. 2 (August 1959), 325–340.

Grimm, Jacob. Review of *Mala Prostonarodnja slaveno-serbska pěsnarica izdana Vukom Stefanovićem*, in *Kleinere Schriften von Jacob Grimm*, Vol. IV. Berlin, 1869. Pp. 427–436.

Humboldt, Wilhelm von. "Ankündigung einer Schrift über die vaskische Sprache und Nation, nebst Angabe des Gesichtspunktes und Inhalts derselben," in *Wilhelm von Humboldts Werke*, Vol. III. Ed. Albert Leitzmann. Berlin, 1904. Pp. 288–299.

Ibrovac, Miodrag. *Kopitar i francuzi*. Beograd, 1953.

Ivić, Aleksa. *Istorija srba u vojvodini*. Novi Sad: Matica srpska, 1929.

Ivić, Milka. "Jedno poređenje vukovog jezika sa našim današnjim književnim jezikom," *Matica srpska, Zbornik za filologiju i lingvistiku*, I (Beograd, 1957), 114–126.

Ivić, Pavle. "O deklinacionim oblicima u srpskohrvatskim dijalektima," *Godišnjak filozofskog fakulteta u Novom Sadu*, IV (Novi Sad, 1959), 189–216.

———. "O govoru galipoljskih srba," *Srpski dijalektološki zbornik*, XII (Beograd, 1957).

———. *Die serbokroatischen Dialekte: ihre Struktur und Entwicklung*, Vol. I: *Allgemeines und die štokavische Dialektgruppe*. The Hague: Mouton and Co., 1958.

Jagić, Vatroslav, ed. *Ènciklopedija slavjanskoj filologii*, Vol. I: *Istorija slavjanskoj filologii*. St. Petersburg, 1910.

———. "Der erste Cetinjer Kirchendruck vom Jahre 1494," *Denkschriften der kaiserlichen Akademie der Wissenschaften, Philosophisch-Historische Classe*, XLIII, no. 2 (Vienna, 1894), 137–180.

Jonke, Ljudevit. *Književni jezik u teoriji i praksi*, 2nd ed. Zagreb: Znanje, 1965.

Jorgović, Aleksandar. "Škole u karlovačkoj mitropoliji," *Jugoslavenska enciklopedija: Narodna enciklopedija srpsko-hrvatsko-slovenačka*, Vol. IV. Ed. Stanoje Stanojević. Zagreb, 1925–1929. Pp. 665–674.

Karadžić, Vuk. *Mala prostonarodnja slaveno-serbska pěsnarica izdana Vukom Stefanovićem*. Vienna, 1814.

———. *Primjeri srpsko-slavenskoga jezika*. Vienna, 1857.

———. *Skupljeni gramatički i polemički spisi*. Ed. L. L. Đorđević. 3 vols. Beograd, 1894, 1896.

———. *Vukova prepiska*. Ed. Ljubomir Stojanović. 7 vols. Beograd, 1908–1913.

Karataev, Ivan. "Opisanie slavjano-russkix knig napečatannyx kirilovskimi bukvami: Tom I: c 1491 po 1652," *Sbornik otdelenija russkago jazyka i slovesnosti imperatorskoj akademii nauk*, XXXIV, no. 2, pp. 1–552 (St. Petersburg, 1883).

Kašić, Jovan. *Jezik Milovana Vidakovića*. Novi Sad: Filozofski fakultet, 1968.

Kidrić, France. *Dobrovský in Slovenski preporod njegove dobe*. Ljubljana, 1930.

Kiselkov, Vasil. *Prouki i očerti po starobългarska literatura*. Sofia: Izd. na bulg. akad. na naukite, 1956.

Kopitar, Bartholomäus. *Grammatik der slavischen Sprache in Krain, Kärnten und Steyermark*. Laibach, 1808.

———. *Kleinere Schriften*, Vol. I. Ed. Franz Miklosich. Vienna, 1857.

———. *Kopitars Briefwechsel mit Karl Georg Rumy*. Ed. Fritz Valjavec. Munich, 1942.

———. *Kopitarjeva spomenica*. Ed. Josip Marn. Ljubljana, 1880.

Kostić, Đorđe. "Principi vukove pravopisne reforme," *Glasnik jugoslovenskog profesorskog društva*, XVIII, nos. 4–5 (Beograd, December 1937—January 1938), 350–361.

———. "Uloga Vuka u stvaranju književnog jezika," *Glasnik jugoslovenskog profesorskog društva*, XVIII, nos. 4–5 (Beograd, December 1937—January 1938), 428–432.

Kovačević, Ljubomir. "Beleške i natpisi," *Glasnik srpskog učenog društva*, LVI (Beograd, 1884), 327–360.

Kulakovskij, Platon. "Načalo russkoj školy u serbov v XVIII v.," *Izvestija otdelenija russkago jazyka i slovesnosti imperatorskoj akademii nauk*, VIII, bk. 2, 246–311; bk. 3, 190–297.

———. *Vuk Karadžič: Ego dejatel'nost' i značenie v serbskoj literature*. Moscow, 1882.

Maretić, Tomislav. *Hrvatski ili srpski jezični savjetnik za sve one, koji žele dobro govoriti i pisati književnim našim jezikom*. Zagreb, 1924.

———. *Gramatika i stilistika hrvatskoga ili srpskoga književnog jezika*. Zagreb, 1899.

Matić, Svetozar. *Naš narodni ep i naš stih: ogledi i studije*. Novi Sad: Matica srpska, 1964.

Mladenović, Aleksandar. *O narodnom jeziku Jovana Rajića*. Novi Sad: Matica srpska, 1964.

Mošin, Vladimir. "O periodizacii russko-južnoslavjanskix literaturnyx svjazej X–XV vv.," *Russkaja literatura XI–XVII vv. sredi slavjanskix literatur. Trudy otdela drevnerusskoj literatury*, XIX. Moscow–Leningrad: Izdatel'stvo Akademii Nauk S.S.S.R., 1963. Pp. 28–106.

Mrazović, Avraam. *Rukovodstvo къ slavenstěj grammaticě ispravlennej vo upotreblenie slaveno-serbskixъ narodnyxъ učilišč, izdano trudomъ Avraama Mrazoviča*, 4th ed. Buda, 1811.

Murko, Mathias. *Die deutsche Einflüsse auf die Anfänge der böhmischen Romantik.* Graz, 1897.

Nikolić, Berislav. "Sremski govor," *Srpski dijalektološki zbornik*, XIV, no. 2 (Beograd, 1964), 207–412.

Novaković, Stojan. *Primeri književnosti i jezika staroga i srpsko-slovenskoga*, 3rd ed. Beograd, 1904.

————. *Srpska bibliografija za noviju književnost.* Beograd, 1869.

————. "Srpski štampari u Rumuniji," *Godišnjica Nikole Čupića*, XVII (Beograd, 1897), 331–348.

Obradović, Dositej. *Dela.* Zagreb: Narodno Delo, 1932.

Pavlović, Milivoj. "Uloga i značaj vojvođanskih pisaca u razvitku srpskoga književnoga jezika," *Zbornik Matice srpske za književnost i jezik*, I (Novi Sad, 1953), 87–100.

Petrovskij, Nestor M. *Pervye gody dejatel'nosti V. Kopitarja.* Kazan', 1906.

————. "Bibliografičeskij spisok trudov V. Kopitarja," *Russkij filologičeskij vestnik*, LXV (Kharkov, 1911), 181–197, 382–399; LXVI, 145–176; LXVII (1912), 189–200.

Poljanec, Franjo. *Istorija srpsko-hrvatskog književnog jezika s pregledom naših dijalekata i istorijskom čitankom*, 3rd ed. Beograd: Narodna Prosveta, 1934.

Popović, Ivan. "Treće lice množine u vojvođanskim govorima," *Zbornik Matice srpske: Serija društvenih nauka*, IV (Novi Sad, 1952), 114–128.

Popović, Miodrag. *Vuk Stefanović Karadžić.* Beograd: Nolit, 1964.

Popović, Pavle. *Jugoslavenska književnost*, 4th ed. Beograd, 1927.

————. *Milovan Vidaković.* Beograd, 1934.

Prodanović, Jaša. "Vuk Karadžić kao kritičar i polemičar," *Glasnik jugoslovenskog profesorskog društva*, XVIII, nos. 4–5 (December 1937–January 1938), 344–349.

Radonić, Jovan. "Atanasije Stojković (1773–1832)," *Glas srpske akademije nauka: Odeljenje društvenih nauka*, CCXII, *Nova serija*, 2 (1953), 97–152.

————. *Slike iz istorije i književnosti.* Beograd, 1938.

Rešetar, Milan. *Der štokavische Dialekt. Kaiserliche Akademie der Wissenschaften: Schriften der Balkankommission, linguistische Abteilung*, Vol. VIII. Vienna, 1907.

Rice, Frank A. *A Study of the Role of Second Languages in Asia, Africa, and Latin America.* Washington D.C.: Center for Applied Linguistics of the M.L.A., 1962.

Ruvarac, Dimitrije. "O prvom štampanom slovenskom bukvaru za srpsku decu," *Godišnjica Nikole Čupića*, XIII (1893), 269–290.

Schlegel, Friedrich von. *Geschichte der alten und neuen Literatur: Kritische Friedrich-Schlegel-Ausgabe*, Vol. VI. Ed. Hans Eichner. Munich-Paderborn-Wien, 1961.

Sinjaver, Leonid. *Žizn' Betxovena.* Moscow: Gosudarstvennoe Muzykal'noe Izdatel'stvo, 1961.

Skerlić, Jovan. *Istorija nove srpske književnosti: Drugo potpuno i ilustrovano izdanje.* Beograd, 1921.

————. *Srpska književnost u XVIII veku. Novo ispravljeno izdanje u redakciji V. Čorovića.* Beograd, 1923.

Sreznevskij, Izmail I. "Vuk Stefanović Karadžić: Biografska i bibliografska skica." Trans. Miloš Moskovljević, *Srpski književni glasnik,* 52 (Beograd, 1937), 383–399.

Stanojević, Stanoje. *Sveti Sava.* Beograd, 1935.

Stojanović, Ljubomir. *Život i rad Vuka Stef. Karadžića.* Beograd, 1924.

————. *Katalog rukopisa i starih štampanih knjiga. Zbirka srpske kraljevske akademije.* Beograd, 1901.

————. *Stari srpski zapisi i natpisi. Zbornik za istoriju, jezik i književnost srpskoga naroda,* Vols. I–III. Beograd, 1902–1905.

Trubeckoj, Nikolaj. *The Common Slavic Element in Russian Culture,* 2nd ed. Ed. Leon Stillman. New York: Columbia University Press, 1952.

Unbegaun, Boris. *Les débuts de la langue littéraire chez les Serbes.* Paris, 1935.

Vasmer, Max. *Bausteine zur Geschichte der deutsch-slavischen geistigen Beziehungen,* Vol. I. Berlin, 1939.

Vidaković, Milovan. *Ljubomir u Elisiumu: romantičeska no pri tom i moralnaja povest'.* 3 vols. Buda, 1814, 1817, 1823.

————. *Usamljeni junoša.* Buda, 1810.

Vinogradov, Viktor. *Očerki po istorii russkogo literaturnogo jazyka XVII–XIX vv.* Leiden: E. I. Brill, 1949.

Vitković, Gavrilo. "Izveštaj, napisao 1733 g. Maksim Radković, eksarh beogradskog mitropolita," *Glasnik srpskog učenog društva,* LVI (Beograd, 1884), 118–285.

Zois, Sigismund. *Korespondenca Sigmunda Barona Zoisa: 1808–1809.* Ed. France Kidrič. Ljubljana, 1939.

THE FALLEN WOMAN IN NINETEENTH CENTURY RUSSIAN LITERATURE

George Siegel

> you highbrow,
> ruffling your matted hair,
> you would thrust upon her
> a sewing machine . . .
> —Majakovskij [1]

Readers of Gogol' will remember the scene in "Nevsky Avenue" in which his two friends, with very different emotions, decide to follow two "fair unknowns" who have just strolled by. A humiliating fate awaits Lieutenant Pirogov who, in lecherous pursuit of his "charming blonde," is manhandled and forcibly stripped. Meanwhile the susceptible and too easily combustible artist, Piskarev, his imagination teeming with fantasies of an impossibly chivalrous love, rushes up the staircase in ardent though platonic pursuit of the other unknown girl. At that moment, "No earthly thought troubled him; no earthly passion blazed within him. No! At that moment he was pure and without stain, like a chaste youth who still yearned for some vague, spiritual love." Alas, she has led him to a brothel, and she herself is a prostitute.

Good God, where had he got to? At first he refused to believe it, and he began scrutinizing the different objects that filled the room. But the bare walls and the uncurtained windows did not indicate the loving care of a housewife, and the faded faces of these wretched creatures, one of whom sat down right in front of him and examined him as coolly as if he were a dirty spot on someone's dress—all that

1. V. M. Mayakovsky, "Back Home!" *The Bedbug and Selected Poetry*, trans. Max Hayward and George Reavey (New York: Meridian Books, 1960), p. 185.

convinced him that he had got to one of those foul places where vice begotten of the spurious education and the terrible overcrowding of a big city takes up its abode, a place where man sacrilegiously crushes and holds up to scorn all that is sacred and pure and all that makes life beautiful, and where woman, the beauty of the world and the crown of creation, becomes a strange and equivocal creature, losing with the purity of her heart all that is womanly and adopting in a way that can only arouse disgust the impudent manners of man, and so ceasing to the the weak and lovely creature that is so different from ourselves . . .

He stood motionless before her and was almost on the point of letting himself be deceived again in a kind of well-meaning, good-natured way as he had let himself be a short while ago, had not the beautiful girl, bored by his long silence, given him a meaning smile, looking straight into his eyes. That smile of hers was full of such pathetic impudence that it was as strange and out of place on her face as a look of piety is on the vicious face of a corrupt official or a ledger in the hands of a poet. He shuddered. She opened those sweet lips of hers and said something, but it was all so stupid, so vulgar . . . He did not want to hear any more. Oh, he was so absurd! He was as simple as a child![2]

In the end the disenchanted Piskarev flees in horror and, unable to reconcile himself to the situation, sinks into a life of dreams and drugs. One dream is particularly radiant; it spurs him to action, to final disillusionment, and to suicide.

Of all his dreams one delighted him more than any other. He dreamt that he was in his studio. He was happy, and it was with real pleasure that he was sitting at his easel with the palette in his hand. And she was there, too. She was his wife. She sat beside him, leaning her sweet little elbow on the back of his chair, and watching him work. Her eyes, languid and heavy, disclosed such a huge load of bliss. Everything in the room breathed of paradise; everything was so bright, so beautifully tidy! O Lord, and now she leaves her sweet little head on his bosom . . . Never had he dreamt a better dream. After it he got up feeling refreshed and less abstracted than before. Strange thoughts came into his head. "Perhaps," he thought, "she has been drawn into her life of vice against her own will by some terrible accident. In her heart of hearts she is perhaps anxious to repent; she is perhaps herself longing to escape from her awful position. And can I suffer her to go to her ruin with callous indifference when all I have to do is

2. V. N. Gogol, *Tales of Good and Evil*, trans. David Magarshack (New York: Doubleday Anchor Books, 1957), pp. 172–175.

to hold out a hand to save her from drowning?" His thoughts went even further. "No one knows me," he said to himself, "and, anyway, no one dares to say anything about me. If she really repents, if she expresses her genuine sorrow and contrition and agrees to change her present way of life, I will marry her. I ought to marry her and I shall probably do much better than any other man who marries his house-keeper or often the most contemptible of creatures. For my action will be wholly disinterested and it may also turn out to be great, since I shall restore to the world one of its beautiful ornaments."

Having conceived this "rather rash plan," he rushes back to the brothel and actually proposes marriage to the prostitute. Fearfully but with "passionate conviction," he explains to her her awful position.

"It's true, I'm poor," said Piskarev at last, after a long and highly instructive homily, "but we will work, we'll do our best, both of us, to improve our position. Surely, nothing can be more agreeable than the feeling that our success will be due entirely to our own efforts. I will do my painting, and you shall sit beside me and inspire me in my work. You can do some embroidering or some other kind of needle-work, and we shall have all we need."

"How do you mean?" she interrupted with an expression of un-disguised scorn. "I'm not a washer woman, or a dress-maker! You don't expect me to work, do you?"

Oh, she could not have described the whole of her mean and con-temptible life better than in those words! A life full of idleness and emptiness, the true companions of vice.[3]

Her response is too much for poor Piskarev. He goes home and cuts his throat.

I have quoted at length from Gogol''s text because of its im-portance. One might even modify the remark attributed to Dostoevskij and suggest that in one way or another all the "literary prostitutes" in nineteenth-century Russian literature come out of "Nevsky Avenue." Brunetière's celebrated remark that of all the influences on literary history, "la principale est celle des oeuvres sur les oeuvres," is especially true here.[4] Of course, this influence is not to be understood as operating in a mechanical way. Nor is it my

---

3. Gogol, *Tales of Good and Evil*, pp. 184–187.
4. Ferdinand Brunetière, *Manuel de l'histoire de la littérature française* (Paris: Delagrave, 1899), p. 4.

intention to give an exhaustive account of the appearance of prostitutes in nineteenth-century Russian literature. Such an endeavor could have statistical significance at best. Rather, I am looking for a literary pattern—a traditional way of treating a literary theme. Although I shall point out a number of parallels, in order to identify a common denominator of the theme, I am aware of the great stylistic divergencies between, for instance, Gogol's "Nevsky Avenue" and Černyševskij's *What's to be Done?*, the poetry of Nekrasov and the stories and novels of Krestovskij, Dostoevskij, Garšin, Tolstoj, Čexov, and Gor'kij.

Turning to an analysis of Gogol's text, one notices at once that the lover, or would-be lover, of the "padšaja ženščina" (fallen woman) is described as innocent, even virginal. In Gogol's words he is "pure and without stain, like a chaste youth," and "simple as a child." Compare this description with the self-characterization of the artist Lopatin in Garšin's "Nadejda Nicolaievna" (1885): "I loved her with the distraction and passion of the first love of a man who has reached twenty-five years of age *without knowing love*."[5] Similarly, the student Vaxljukov in Vsevolod Krestovskij's "Pogibšee, no miloe sozdanie" (A Dear But Fallen Creature, 1864) shuns "the seamstresses and milliners from the second-rate shops; his heart was free and not one district dulcinea had touched it."[6] The embarrassed seventeen-year-old student in Nadson's sketch "Slezy" (Tears, 1882) puts the matter very simply: "'It's'—and his voice dropped—'it's the first time for me.'"[7]

The fallen woman herself is depicted by Gogol' in a vague and cloudy way, which seems typical of his descriptions of women in general. Besides an aura of "romance," the characterization includes stylized elements of "boldness" and "immorality." The conventionality of Gogol's description is underlined by his use of pleasant but empty expressions: "she stood before him as *beautiful* as ever; her hair was as *lovely*; her eyes seemed no whit less *heavenly*

5. W. M. Garshin, *The Signal and Other Stories*, trans. Captain Rowland Smith (New York: Alfred A. Knopf, 1915), p. 205 (my italics).

6. V. Krestovskij, *Sobranie sočinenij* (St. Petersburg: Obščestvennaja Pol'za, 1899), II, 633. Krestovskij's title is a quotation from Puškin's *Pir vo vremja čumy* (*The Feast During the Plague, 1831*). Unless otherwise indicated, all translations are my own.

7. S. J. Nadson, *Proza, dnevniki, pis'ma* (St. Petersburg, 1912), p. 446.

... the *beautiful* girl who had bewitched poor Piskarev was indeed a most *extraordinary* and *singular* phenomenon ... Her features were so *faultlessly formed*, the whole expression of her *lovely* face was marked by such *nobility*, that it was impossible to believe that vice had already got its terrible claws into her." [8]

The abstract and hackneyed quality of Gogol''s description finds its counterpart in Garšin's "Nadejda Nicolaievna." The epithets have been inverted, but the effect is the same. Garšin describes his heroine as having a "stern and almost cruel expression." In her voice he finds a ring of "wounded pride," while her glance is "scornful, even insolent." When she poses as a model, her soul is "proud and unhappy"; her face expresses "determination and longing, pride and fear, love and hate." [9]

Gogol''s stress on the romantic beauty of the fallen woman is for the most part dropped by later writers, although its echo persists in Krestovkij's "Pogibšee, no miloe sozdanie." The shy student oɪ mathematics collides with an "unknown" one winter night in St. Petersburg: "A rather young and extremely beautiful girl stood before him. Her expressive, black gazelle-like eyes gazed up at him tenderly and then she smiled. In his sentimental moments he had dreamt of such a smile. It was a smile that combined welcome, interest, and affection, and there was a touch of tender concern, too." [10]

On the other hand, those elements of Gogol''s characterization that emphasize the "vicious" brazenness of the fallen woman and contrast this quality sentimentally with her innocent exterior are taken up by succeeding writers. Recall that the chaste, abstemious Piskarev is shocked when his "fallen woman" tells him that she was "dead drunk." As Gogol' remarks elsewhere with a slight quaver: "She was only seventeen!" So, too, the hero of Krestovskij's "Pogibšee, no miloe sozdanie" is shocked to find his "purest ideal" with her "gazelle-like eyes" dancing the can-can. And Nadežda Nikolaevna, as she appears in Garšin's earlier tale "An Incident" (1878), dresses up as a "respectable girl" to meet her "poor but honest" suitor, but then is horrified when she looks in the mirror:

8. Gogol, *Tales of Good and Evil*, pp. 174–175 (my italics).
9. Garshin, "*Nadejda Nicolaievna*," p. 184.
10. Krestovskij, "Pogibšee, no miloe sozdanie," p. 633.

"I almost cried out at seeing in it a woman not at all like the Evgenia who performs indecent dances so well at various cafés. It was not the impudent, beringed cocotte with smiling face, flashy puffed-out chignon and pencilled lashes. This draggled and suffering woman, pale-faced and melancholy-looking, with big black eyes and dark circles around them, is something quite new—it is not I."[11]

A similar emphasis on the "brazenness" of the fallen woman occurs again in Černyševskij's *What's To Be Done?* although the treatment of the theme is much different in spirit. The conventionally shameless elements in the characterization make for a good deal of humor in the woman's account of one adventure:

> I was walking along Nevsky Avenue: I had just gone out, and it was still early; I saw a student coming, and directed my steps toward him. He did not say a word, but simply crossed to the other side of the street. I followed him, and grasped him by the arm. "No," I said to him, "I will not leave you, you are so fine looking."
> "But I beg you to leave me," said he.
> "Oh, no; come with me."
> "I have no reason to."
> "Well, I will go with you. Where are you going? For nothing in the world will I leave you." I was impudent, as impudent as any and more so ... So I went, talking all sorts of nonsense to him: but he said not a word ... I stretched myself upon the divan and said:
> "Some wine!"
> "No," said he, "I shall not give you any wine; only tea, provided you want it."
> "With punch," said I.
> "No, without punch."
> I began to act riotously.[12]

The mythical pattern of the prostitute is completed when she is "rehabilated," domesticated and made respectable. True, in Gogol''s story, Piskarev's desire to rehabilitate the fallen woman is characterized as "a somewhat rash plan", and the comical adventure of Lieutenant Pirogov provides an ironic accompaniment to the tragic story of the artist. The sentimentality of the story is thus attenuated, and the final impression left by "Nevsky Avenue" is one of playful

11. Garshin, "An Incident," p. 42.
12. N. G. Tchernyshevsky, *What's To Be Done*, trans. Benjamin Tucker (Boston: B. R. Tucker, 1886), pp. 164–165.

irony. But the theme of the rehabilitation of a fallen woman, presenting its rich opportunities for the literary display of pity and altruism, was eagerly adopted by the writers who followed Gogol'. It meshed well with the zeitgeist, with the period's taste for philanthropic literature and compassion for the downtrodden. Nekrasov made this theme the subject of a famous poem, "When from thy error, dark, degrading" (1845), which in very different ways was to influence Dostoevskij and Černyševskij:

> When from thine error, dark, degrading,
> With words of fiery persuading,
> I drew thy fallen spirit out;
> And thou, thy hands in anguish wringing,
> Didst curse, filled with a torment stinging,
> The sin that compassed thee about;
> When thou, thy conscience dilatory
> Chastising with the memory's shame,
> Didst there unfold to me the story
> Of that which was before I came;
> And sudden with thy two hands shielding
> In loathing and dismay thy face,
> To floods of tears I saw thee yielding,
> O'erwhelmed, yea prostrate with disgrace—
> Trust me! thy tale did not importune;
> I caught each word and tired not.
> I understood, child of misfortune!
> I pardoned all, and all forgot.
> Why is it then, a secret doubting
> Still preys upon thee every hour?
> The world's opinion, thoughtless flouting,
> Holds even thee too in its power?
> Heed not the world, its lies dissembling,
> Henceforth from thy doubts be free;
> Nor let thy soul, unduly trembling,
> Still harbor thoughts that torture thee.
> By grieving fruitlessly and vainly
> Warm not the serpents in thy breast,
> Into my house come bold and free,
> Its rightful mistress there to be.[13]

13. "When from thine error, dark, degrading," trans. Archibald Carey Coolidge, *The Harvard Monthly*, 19: 133 (Jan. 1895). I have altered the last two lines of the translation to correspond to the translation in "Notes from Underground."

The second line of the poem—"With words of fiery persuading" —corresponds to Piskarev's harangue in the brothel: "he began explaining her awful position to her in a voice that shook, but which was at the same time full of passionate conviction." But the characteristic difference is that this time the sermon is successful, the fallen woman is properly contrite, and the man is all-forgiving. All Gogolian irony has vanished. Nekrasov's poem is a piece of rhetoric, with a touch of wounding condescension. It is scarcely surprising that the poem created a stir in radical circles, or that Černyševskij wrote to Nekrasov that the verse had made him "literally sob." [14]

The literary pattern for the regeneration of the fallen woman, lightly sketched in "Nevsky Avenue," is fully developed by Nekrasov. The speaker of the poem lectures on vice and the necessity for reform. The girl shudders at her past, "tells all," and with the help of the man's magnanimity the "child of misfortune" is transformed into the "rightful mistress" of the house. Between the confession and the happy ending the girl is given over to secret doubt and oppressed by false conventional standards ("the world's opinion"), though admonished by the hero not to heed the mendacious and empty opinions of the crowd.

The situation roughly corresponds to Garšin's "An Incident," in which the hero wonders if Nadežda Nilolaevna knows that "there is a man who would consider it happiness to sit with her in a room, and only look into her eyes, not even touching her hands. That there is a man who would hurl himself into the fire if it would help her to get out of the hell in which she lives, if she wanted to get out of it? But she does not." [15] The motif of rehabilitation is reiterated by the artist Lopatin in Garšin's "Nadejda Nicolaievna": "I longed to snatch her away from the horrors which were tormenting her, to take her in my arms somewhere far, far away, to fondle and press her to my heart, so that she might forget, so as to bring a smile on her suffering face." [16] Although Nadežda Nikolaevna is very much aware that Nikitin wishes "to make an honest woman of her," she is tormented by pride and secret doubts, in the spirit of Nekrasov's poem.

14. For an obvious imitation of Nekrasov's poem, see N. A. Dobroljubov, *Stixotvorenija* (Leningrad: Sovetskij pisatel', 1941), p. 58.
15. Garshin, "An Incident," pp. 34–35.
16. Garshin, "Nadejda Nicolaievna," p. 205.

"Am I sorry for him? No. What can I do for him? Marry him? Dare I? Would it not be the same selling of myself? Yes—no, it would be even worse!"

She did not know why it would be worse, but felt it.

"Now, I am at least frank. Anyone may strike me. Have I not suffered insults? But then, how would I be better? Would it not be the same depravity, only less frank? . . . It seems to me that if I let this man get the upper hand of me he will torment me with recollections . . . and I could not endure it . . . I do not know myself why I do not wish to take advantage of this opportunity to have done with this awful life, to rid myself of this nightmare. If I were to marry him? A new life, new hopes . . .

"But no! Now he is ready to lick my hand, but afterwards will trample me underfoot and say: 'And you still oppose me, contemptible creature! You despise me!'

"Would he say this? I think so." [17]

The attempted reformation of the fallen woman ends in the hero's suicide in "An Incident"; in "Nadejda Nicolaievna" the finale is equally violent, with two murders and the hero on his deathbed. One Russian writer, however, who was directly influenced by Nekrasov's poem found a less melodramatic solution to the problem of the fallen woman. Černyševskij's *What's To Be Done?* was wittily described by Georg Brandes as "a sort of bastard between a novel and a treatise on political economy; it descends on the female side from George Sand and on the male from Karl Marx." [18] In justice to Černyševskij, it should be said that his treatment of the fallen woman theme is much less sentimental and rhetorical than are some others.

Natas'ja Krjukova, who works as a seamstress in a cooperative shop, has had a shady past. "I was a very wicked girl, Vera Pavlovna . . . And I was very insolent; I had no shame, and was always drunk . . . As to the life that I led, of course there is no occasion to speak of it; it is always the same with poor women of that sort." [19] She then relates her encounter with the medical student Kirsanov. Kirsanov himself is in Černyševskij's description one of the "new men (novye ljudi)—bold and resolute, knowing what to do under all circumstances, and doing it with a strong arm when necessary."

17. Garshin, "An Incident," pp. 38–39.
18. Georg Brandes, *Impressions of Russia*, trans. Samuel C. Eastman (New York: Thomas Y. Crowell and Co., 1889), p. 268.
19. Tchernyshevsky, *What's To Be Done*, p. 164.

4—H.S.S.

Such men may be chaste by choice, Černyševskij remarks, but they are quite capable of carrying on an amorous intrigue with perfect sang-froid. Kirsanov's friend Lopuxov is a man of precisely this stamp. In spite of his abstemious life in other respects as a medical student, he manages to enjoy many liaisons. He becomes enamored of a dancing girl, who is attracted by his good looks and air of resolution, and consents to be his mistress for a fortnight. The relationship terminates amicably on both sides. Lopuxov's character contrasts sharply to the idealistic, dreamy, virginal, and chivalrous lover of the fallen woman.

His "gallant adventure" also contrasts with Kirsanov's encounter with Nastas'ja Krjukova. In dry prose, Černyševskij describes Krjukova's visit to Kirsanov's lodgings. The medical student maintains his equanimity in the face of her provocative behavior, serves her tea instead of the wine she asks for, speaks to her politely without condescension, using "vy" instead of "ty," and, in his professional capacity as a doctor, examines her chest. He finds her tubercular, advises her to abandon a mode of life that forces her to drink, and pays her debts to the madame of the brothel where she has been working. A new life actually begins for Nastas'ja Krjukova, portrayed unromantically and with a genuine tenderness:

> I freed myself from my mistress and hired a little room. But there was nothing that I could do: in freeing us they give us a special kind of certificate; where could I turn with such a document? And I had no money. Consequently I lived as before, though not exactly as before. I received only my best acquaintances, those not offensive to me; wine I left alone. What was the difference, then, you ask? My life was already much less distressing than it had been. But it was still distressing, and let me tell you something: you will think that it was distressing because I had many friends, five perhaps; no, for I felt an affection for all of them, hence it was not that . . . Today I am still of the same mind: if you feel affection, there is no harm, provided there is no deceit; if there is deceit that is another thing.[20]

To go from a brothel to a private apartment where one sees only five favorite clients is also, of course, a realistic step up the social ladder. Such an action would be aesthetically inconceivable in the "romantic" world of Gogol' or Garšin.

20. Tchernyshevsky, *What's To Be Done*, p. 167.

Kirsanov visits Natas'ja Krjukova from time to time, helps to support her in her efforts to abstain from liquor, and treats her generally as though she were his patient. Then one day he declares his love, at which point the prose becomes rather sugary ("you are now a virtuous girl"). They live together happily for only two years, separating because her tuberculosis has become acute. When they meet again two years later, Kirsanov, who recognizes that Krjukova has not long to live, acts purely from motives of compassion and decides to stay with her till the end. Černyševskij again provides a "realistic" rationale:

> it is needless to say that the feeling of Kirsanov toward the young Krjukova, at the time of their second coming together, was not analogous to that of her toward him. He no longer loved her; he was only well disposed toward her, as one is toward a woman whom one has loved. His old love for her had been no more than a youth's desire to love someone, no matter whom. It is needless to say that Nasten'ka was never fitted for him, for they were not equals in intellectual development. When he grew to be more than a youth, he could no more than pity her; he could be kind to her for memory's and compassion's sake, and that was all.[21]

Černyševskij might sob over Nekrasov's sentimentally rhetorical verse, but he preserved a hard-headedness when it actually came to his treating the problem of the fallen woman.

The first number of Dostoevskij's journal *Èpoxa* included Vsevolod Krestovskij's story "Pogibšee, no miloe sozdanie," alluded to earlier as preserving many features that derive from Gogol''s prototype. Written in a painfully arch tone and obviously aping "Nevsky Avenue," the story relates the adventures of a fallen woman and the inevitable student. The young man is haunted by the smile and eyes of a girl he has bumped into on the street. He searches for her in vain, till one night he hears the sound of a Strauss waltz coming from a nearby house. Looking through the window, he sees a "ravishingly charming," curly-haired baby asleep on a sofa, while on the opposite side of the room the girl is playing the piano. The lexicon of this story, with its glances that are "so kind, so warm, so sympathetic," its smiles that are "so timid, so charming," filled with "affection and

21. Tchernyshevsky, *What's To Be Done*, pp. 171–172.

welcome," "interest and tender concern," would have aroused Karamzin's envy. Typical is a scene in a German-style beer garden where the student mistakes the "mysterious stranger's" escort for her cousin, as well as that extraordinary emotional outburst which occurs when, having lost sight of his "ideal," he suddenly finds her again: "What do I want? . . . My God! . . . Listen, I love you! I love you insanely. Forgive me but it's true . . . Recall our very first meeting before Spring, recall that night when you saw me from your window, recall how I have followed you like a shadow till just recently. O, don't drive me away, don't drive me away! No one has ever smiled at me the way you have; no one has ever looked at me with such kind, such holy eyes . . . O thank you for that!" The mysterious stranger attempts to calm him. Would he like to hear music? "Yes, yes! Music! Melodies! O, let me hear melodies! I have not heard any in ever so long . . . Only permit me to stay under your window and listen—I ask nothing more." [22]

The denouement is musical too, only this time the score is not Strauss but Offenbach. In a shady dance hall the student recognizes his "Saint Cecelia" dancing the can-can. Since the student still does not know who she is, having met her only for fleeting moments, an onlooker presents him with the girl's full dossier:

> Who is she? A sinner, just like all the others here. . . . She started out as a modest "forget-me-not," lived with some chap who was getting on in years "all for love" . . . they say he seduced her and then as is usual in these cases abandoned her . . . Es ist eine alte Geschichte . . . Now, she's a candidate for the violet class or perhaps the camelia . . . I am always struck by the contrast between her virginal face and her depraved life . . . Still, I'm sorry for the poor thing . . . She was unhappy with that older chap, he was jealous, he tormented her . . . and in the end he abandoned her and their daughter. What a swine! . . . But look at her, who would think she has a daughter. Just watch her doing the can-can. [23]

The student is plunged in despair, hope gone, ideals shattered. But he cannot accept the situation as it stands. He must have an explanation with her. Obtaining her address, he rushes to her house "with sinking heart." In the final paragraph Krestovskij, discarding the

22. Krestovskij, "Pogibšee, no miloe sozdanie," p. 643.
23. Krestovskij, "Pogibšee, no miloe sizdanie," p. 644.

music of Strauss and Offenbach, invokes the spirit of Brahms' *Lullaby*: "In front of him was a cozy little room, faintly illuminated by the full light of a night-lamp . . . there stood a tiny narrow crib with muslin bed-curtains thrown back . . . and there, on her knees, leaning tenderly over the head of the crib was *she*—his virginal, Saint Cecelia, still wearing the splendid attire in which she had danced so brazenly an hour before . . . Now those gentle beautiful eyes expressed the most lofty, the most sacred maternal love . . . and two large, warm tears glittered on that exaltedly mournful countenance."[24]

Although today Krestovskij's story seems hopelessly banal, trite, and sentimental, Dostoevskij, in selecting it for the first issue of his new journal *Èpoxa*, must have considered it a serious contribution to the problem of the fallen woman. In any case, the problem of prostitution was very fashionable at the moment: Nekrasov himself was the editor of *Sovremennik*, the most influential literary journal of the time. The humanitarian novels of George Sand and Victor Hugo, with their sympathy for the downtrodden and the oppressed, were immensely popular in Russia and had become part of the moral atmosphere. More specifically, Victor Hugo in his lush prose had become a champion of the fallen woman.[25] He depicted "virtuous

24. Krestovskij, "Pogibšee, no miloe sozdanie," p. 646.
25. Nekrasov's poem may be compared with a French counterpart of 1835 by Victor Hugo:

> Oh! n'insultez jamais une femme qui tombe!
> Qui sait sous quel fardeau la pauvre âme succombe?
> Qui sait combien de jours sa faim a combattu?
> Quand le vent du malheur ébranlait leur vertu,
> Qui de nous n'a pas vu de ces femmes brisées
> S'y cramponner longtemps de leurs mains épuisées!
> Comme au bout d'une branche on voit étinceler
> Une goutte de pluie ou le ciel vient briller,
> Qu'on secoue avec l'arbre et qui tremble et qui lutte,
> Perle avant de tomber en fange après sa chute!
> La faute en est à nous. A toi, riche! à ton or!
> Cette fange d'ailleur contient l'eau pure encor.
> Pour que la goutte d'eau sorte de la poussière,
> Et redevienne perle en sa splendeur première,
> Il suffit, c'est ainsi que tout remonte au jour,
> d'un rayon de soleil on d'un rayon d'amour!

Victor Hugo, *Oeuvres Complètes de Victor Hugo*, vol. III, *Poésie* (Paris: J. Hetzel and Co., 1888), p. 38.

prostitutes," such as Paquette in *Notre Dame de Paris* (1831) and Fantine in *Les Misérables* (1862). With typical French sentimentality, Hugo endowed his fallen creatures with swollen maternal passions—a possible reflection of which appears in Krestovskij's "Pogibšee, no miloe sozdanie." Sonja Marmeladova in Dostoevskij's *Crime and Punishment*, who goes "on the streets" for the sake of a starving family, undoubtedly springs from the same genealogical tree. I. I. Jasinskij's *Nataška* (1881) is another example of the type: its seventeen-year old heroine tries to be a prostitute in order to feed the family but, unable to go through with it, freezes to death on the St. Petersburg streets.

A literary pattern or convention inevitably leads to a literary reaction—to satire, parody, or criticism. It is against the background of the sentimental humanitarianism typified by writers like Hugo and Nekrasov that one must picture Dostoevskij's "Notes from Underground" (1864). The story, as Victor Šklovskij has observed, is profoundly dualistic in structure. On the one hand, Dostoevskij uses his underground man as a mouthpiece for his own polemics against Černyševskij's *What's To Be Done?* and the ideological position taken by Nekrasov's journal *Sovremennik*; on the other hand, the underground man himself is exposed by his own doubts and vacillations.[26] It is interesting to compare the second part of "Notes from Underground," entitled "Apropos of the Wet Snow," with the chapter "Krjukova's Story" in *What's To Be Done?* Krjukova, Černyševskij's fallen woman, loves the medical student Kirsanov. Liza, Dostoevskij's fallen woman, keeps as her most cherished possession, a letter from a medical student, which she shows to the underground man. Both Liza and Krjukova have "weak" chests and are threatened with tuberculosis. Krjukova and Kirsanov have two meetings, which are paralleled by the two meetings of Liza and the underground man. However, whereas Kirsanov drily advises Krjukova to leave the brothel and gives her money to pay her debts, the underground man indulges in a sadistic harangue at the expense of the defenseless girl, whose very name recalls another unfortunate Nikolaj Karamzin's "Poor Liza." As a final gesture, after Liza has

26. Viktor Šklovskij, *Za i protiv* (Moscow: Sovetskij pisatel', 1957), pp. 126–165. I have leaned heavily on Šklovskij's discussion of "Notes from Underground" and have borrowed freely from his interpretation.

given herself to him in an access of compassion, which is intolerable to the vanity of the underground man, he insultingly presses money on her. Kirsanov and the underground man are contrasted in their ways of dealing with an officer who blocks their way on a city street: the resolute Kirsanov knocks him into the gutter; the underground man slinks away and dreams of avenging himself by publishing a satire. Šklovskij is thus undoubtedly correct in asserting that "Apropos of the Wet Snow," if not a parody of "Krjukova's Story," is ironically and antithetically juxtaposed to it.

The "enlightened socialism" of Černyševskij is one target of Dostoevskij's story; Nekrasov's rhetorical "humanitarianism" is the other, and precisely as it is expressed in Nekrasov's poem on the fallen woman. Before Doestoevskij wrote "Notes from Underground," he had already begun to mock Nekrasov's poem in "The Friend of the Family" (1859), in which he put the following speech in the mouth of the simple-minded narrator:

> And I began fervently declaring that even in the creature who has fallen lowest there may still survive the finest human feelings; that the depths of the human soul are unfathomable; that we must not despise the fallen, but on the contrary ought to seek them out and raise them up; that the commonly accepted standard of goodness and morality was not infallible, and so on, and so on; in fact, I warmed up to the subject, and even began talking about the realist school. In conclusion I even repeated the verses: "When from thy error, dark, degrading.[27]

Note particularly the two "and so on's." This device is undoubtedly used to suggest that the sentiments in question are banal, stereotyped, and cliché. The same device is used in "Notes from Underground." Nekrasov's poem is given as an epigraph to the second part, but it is purposely cut off at the fourteenth line, followed by three etceteras. Dostoevskij writes "From the verse of N. A. Nekrasov." The last two lines of Nekrasov's poem are quoted twice: in the middle of Chapter VIII, where they are again closely followed by a string of etceteras, and as an epigraph to Chapter IX, where in place of Nekrasov's signature Dostoevskij writes, "from the same verse." Both instances deserve examination.

27. F. M. Dostoevsky, "The Friend of the Family," *The Short Novels of Dostoevsky* (New York: Dial Press, 1951), p. 803.

The situation at the beginning of Chapter VIII reveals the underground man in terror that the prostitute Liza will visit him as a result of his eloquent sermon in the brothel. He assumes that on that occasion he appeared to her like a hero, but wonders what she would think of him now, in his cheap lodgings with his grubby dressing gown. His vanity makes this thought unbearable. When at last he convinces himself that she will not come, he breathes freely and even amuses himself with fantasies of rescuing her and making her his wife, *à la* Nekrasov:

> I, for instance, become the salvation of Liza, simply through her coming to me and my talking to her . . . I develop her, educate her. Finally, I notice that she loves me, loves me passionately. I pretend not to understand (I don't know, however, why I pretend, just for effect, perhaps). At last all confusion, transfigured, trembling and sobbing, she flings herself at my feet and says that I am her saviour, and that she loves me better than anything in the world. I am amazed, but . . .
>
> "Liza," I say, "can you imagine that I have not noticed your love? I saw it all, I divined it, but I did not dare to approach you first, because I had an influence over you and was afraid that you would force yourself, from gratitude, to respond to my love, would try to rouse in your heart a feeling which was perhaps absent, and I did not wish that . . . because it would be tyranny . . . it would be indelicate (in short, I launch off at that point into European, inexplicably lofty subtleties à la George Sand) but now, now you are mine, you are my creation, you are pure, you are good, you are my noble wife.
>
> > "Into my house come bold and free,
> > Its rightful mistress there to be."
>
> Then we begin living together, go abroad, and so on, and so on. In fact, in the end it seemed vulgar to me myself, and I began putting out my tongue at myself.[28]

This blatant parody on the humanitarian principles of Nekrasov's poem is made even more sardonic by the fact that the underground man ventures on such fantasies only after he is certain that Liza will not intrude on him and he will be spared the necessity of doing anything. It is clear that Dostoevskij is here reducing Nekrasov's rhetoric on the fallen woman to an onanistic indulgence.

28. Dostoevsky, "Notes from Underground," *The Short Novels of Dostoevsky*, pp. 207–208.

Dostoevskij, one of the most brutal of writers, was extraordinarily sensitive to brutality in others. He saw through the veil of humanitarian feelings a scarcely concealed condescension in Nekrasov's poem. Who was to look down on whom? Was a "liberal," "progressive," or "radical" writer from the editorial office of the *Sovremennik* to patronize a poor prostitute? Was this the way to show "humanitarian principles"? Dostoevskij answered the "humanitarians" in "Notes from Underground."

Yet it would be an error to conclude that Dostoevskij was attacking only the contemporary rhetoric of humanitarianism. For him, the problem was essentially a moral one, and a businessman's condescension was as evil as a humanitarian's. This is brought out in the scene in *Crime and Punishment* (1866) in which the businessman Lužin dreams voluptuously of marriage to a "poor defenseless girl":

> For many years he had voluptuous dreams of marriage, but he had gone on waiting and amassing money. He brooded with relish . . . over the image of a girl . . . one who had suffered much, and was completely humbled before him, one who would all her life look on him as her saviour, worship him, admire him and only him. How many scenes, how many amorous episodes he had imagined on this seductive and playful theme, when his work was over!—her helpless position had been a great allurement . . . and this creature would be slavishly grateful all her life for his heroic condescension, and would humble herself in the dust before him, and he would have absolute, unbounded power over her![29]

It is true that Lužin wishes to marry a "virtuous" girl, but his attitude is fundamentally the same as that of the would-be benefactors of fallen women.

The sadism of the sermons of such benefactors is expressed by Dostoevskij in the scene in which the underground man visits Liza at the brothel. Provoked by her silence, he tries "to get at her soul" through sentimentally cruel descriptions of happy family life. He pointedly contrasts these rosy pictures with Liza's actual position, and torments her with the ominous possibilities of the future:

29. Dostoevsky, *Crime and Punishment* (New York: The Modern Library, 1944), pp. 301–302.

You will change to another house, then to a third, then somewhere else, till you come down at last to the Haymarket. There you will be beaten at every turn; that is good manners there, the visitors don't know how to be friendly without beating you. You don't believe that it is so hateful there? Go and look for your self some time, you can see with your own eyes. Once, one New Year's Day, I saw a woman at a door. They had turned her out as a joke, to give her a taste of the frost because she had been crying so much, and they shut the door behind her. At nine o'clock in the morning she was already quite drunk, dishevelled, half-naked, covered with bruises, her face was powdered, but she had a black eye, blood was trickling from her nose and teeth; some cabman had just given her a drubbing. She was sitting on the stone steps, a salt fish of some sort was in her hand; she was crying, wailing something about her luck and beating with the fish on the steps, and cabmen and drunken soldiers were crowding in the doorway taunting her.[30]

The underground man, who is chiefly afraid of being laughed at, has embarked on these rhetorical flights partly to get the upper hand, since for him all encounters are competitions, and partly for the sheer pleasure of manipulating another's personality.

When Liza visits him, looking for help, in that harrowing scene which is ironically prefaced by the last two lines of Nekrasov's poem, the underground man turns on her in hysterical fury:

"Save you!" I went on, jumping up from my chair and running up and down the room before her. "Save you from what? But perhaps I am worse than you myself. Why didn't you throw it in my teeth when I was giving you that sermon: 'But what did you come here yourself for? Was it to read us a sermon?' Power, power was what I wanted then, sport was what I wanted, I wanted to wring out your tears, your humiliation, your hysteria—that was what I wanted then! Of course, I couldn't keep it up then, because I am a wretched creature, I was frightened, and, the devil knows why, gave you my address in my folly. Afterwards, before I got home, I was cursing and swearing at you because of that address, I hated you already because of the lies I had told you. Because I only like playing with words, only dreaming, but, do you know, what I really want is that you should all go to hell. That is what I want. I want peace; yes, I'd sell the whole world for a farthing, straight off, so long as I was left in peace. Is the world to go to pot, or am I to go without my tea? I say the world may go to pot for me, so long as I always get my tea. Did you know that, or not? Well, anyway, I know that I am a blackguard, a scoundrel, an egoist,

30. Dostoevsky, "Notes from Underground," p. 200.

a sluggard. Here I have been shuddering for the last three days at the thought of your coming. And do you know what has worried me particularly for these three days? That I posed as such a hero to you, and now you would see me in a wretched, torn dressing-gown, beggarly, loathsome." [31]

In this frenzied, harrowing monologue—one of the most brilliant in Russian literature—Dostoevskij has stood Nekrasov on his head. The penitent woman, the sobbing, shame-faced, and guilty fallen woman, has been replaced by the emotionally lacerated man. It is he who confesses, writhing before her in a paroxysm of guilt and self-reproach. This brilliant reversal is undoubtedly a part of Dostoevskij's attack on "Russian romanticism," about which he makes withering comments in the first part of the story. The romantic hero has become the anti-hero par excellence, while the whore has become the symbol of humanity. Thus, by exalting the woman and debasing the man, Dostoevskij has injected a genuine ethical seriousness into a banal theme.

The exaltation of the fallen woman, which is implicit in "Notes from Underground," has become an outright apotheosis in the novel *Crime and Punishment*. The portrait of Sonja Marmeladova teeters precariously on the edge of sentimentality. Dostoevskij gives a realistic motivation for his glorification of the fallen woman by introducing Sonja through the medium of Marmeladov's drunken monologue, in which maudlin sentimentality would seem natural. Yet when the drunken, guilty father invokes the spirit of Christ, a strain is evident, very close to the lachrymose: "but He will pity us Who has had pity on all men, Who has understood all men and all things, He is the one, He too is the Judge. He will come in that day and He will ask: 'Where is the daughter who gave herself for her cross, consumptive stepmother and for the little children of another? Where is the daughter who had pity upon the filthy drunkard, her earthly father, undismayed by his beastliness?" [32]

Unlike Dostoevskij's treatment of the fallen woman, Tolstoj''s is relatively free from sentimental exaltation. The fallen woman in *Anna Karenina* (1877) is described simply and without rhetorical flourish. Early in the novel Levin visits his sick and broken brother

31. Dostoevsky, "Notes from Underground," pp. 215–216.
32. Dostoevsky, *Crime and Punishment*, pp. 23–24.

Nikolaj, who in a gesture of defiance presents his mistress to him: "'And this woman,' Nikolay Levin interrupted him, pointing to her, 'is the partner of my life, Marya Nikolaevna. I took her out of a bad house,' and he jerked his neck saying this, 'but I love her and respect her, and any one who wants to know me,' he added, raising his voice and knitting his brows, 'I beg to love her and respect her. She's just the same as my wife, just the same. So now you know whom you've got to do with. And if you think you're lowering yourself, well, here's the floor, there's the door.'" [33] Levin answers pacifyingly that there can be no question of "lowering himself," but the possibility that his wife Kitty might come in contact with Mar'ja Nikolaevna plainly unnerves him: "the mere idea of his wife, his Kitty, being in the same room with a common wench set him shuddering with horror and loathing." Levin meets Mar'ja Nikolaevna once more when his brother is dying, and Tolstoj's description of the scene is again sober and realistic: "He went out of the door without a word, and at once stumbled over Marya Nikolaevna, who had heard of his arrival and had not dared to go in to see him. She was just the same as when he saw her in Moscow; the same woolen gown, and bare arms and neck, and the same good-naturedly stupid, pock-marked face, only a little plumper." [34]

One might say that it is Nikolaj rather than Mar'ja Nikolaevna who takes on the functions of a fallen woman in Tolstoj's account. It is he who falls socially and morally: "All the long way to his brother's, Levin vividly recalled all the facts familiar to him of his brother Nikolay's life. He remembered how his brother, while at the university and for a year afterwards, had, in spite of the jeers of his companions, lived like a monk, strictly observing all religious rites, services, and fasts, and avoiding every sort of pleasure, especially women. And afterwards, how he had all at once broken out: he had associated with the most horrible people, and rushed into the most senseless debauchery." [35]

Tolstoj presents a full-scale portrait of a fallen woman in his novel *Resurrection* (1899). The plot turns somewhat wearily on the

33. Leo Tolstoy, *Anna Karenina*, trans. Constance Garnett (New York: World Publishing Company, 1946), p. 110.

34. Tolstoy, *Anna Karenina*, pp. 556–557.

35. Tolstoy, *Anna Karenina*, pp. 107–108.

seduction of the young maid-servant Maslova by a thoughtless nobleman, Nekhljudov. She is cruelly deserted by him and drifts into prostitution. Her seducer is a juryman at the trial where she is falsely accused of murder. He recognizes her, his conscience awakens, and unable to have her sentence commuted, he follows her to prison and exile in Siberia.

Čexov once said that the least interesting aspect of this novel was the relations between Maslova and Nekhljudov, and his criticism has merit.[36] It is difficult to share Tolstoj's interest in Nekhljudov's attempts to right an old wrong. One feels with Maslova that Nekhljudov is most concerned with saving his own soul. Like other lovers of the fallen woman, Nekhljudov expects to find Maslova grateful for his repentance and his efforts to help her. He wants her to be ashamed and contrite, in accordance with the requirements of the literary convention of the fallen woman: "What surprised him most was that she showed no sign of shame, except as a prisoner: she was very much ashamed of being in gaol—but of being a prostitute, not at all. On the contrary, she seemed rather pleased with herself and proud of her position." Nekhljudov, who sees in Maslova his passport to salvation, continues to importune her. Finally, she turns on him in rage and exposes the moral insincerity of the repentant nobleman's actions: "'Go away! I'm a convict and you are a prince—you have no business to be here!' she said, her face distorted with rage, pulling away her hand. 'You want to save yourself through me,' she went on rapidly, as though in haste to pour out every feeling in her heart. 'You had your pleasure from me, and now you want to get your salvation through me. I loathe you, and your spectacles, and your fat disgusting face! Clear out!' she shouted, springing to her feet."[37]

That Maslova will again feel love for Nekhljudov but decides not to marry him because the marriage would be his ruin is beside the point. *Resurrection* is concerned not with the reformation of a fallen woman, but with the reformation of Nekhljudov. The novel ends with a medley of quotations from the Gospels, and it is clear that

36. Anton Chekhov, *The Selected Letters of Anton Chekhov*, ed. Lillian Hellman (New York: Farrar Straus and Company, 1955), p. 263.

37. Tolstoy, *Resurrection*, trans. Vera Trail (New York: Pantheon, 1956), pp. 110, 189.

Tolstoj-Nekhljudov is looking for a way out of his inevitable aristo-
cratic isolation.

The rehabilitation of fallen women played a curious rôle in
Vsevolad Garšin's life as well as in his art. His younger brother,
Viktor, is said to have committed suicide because of a romantic and
hopeless love for a prostitute. He himself gained a reputation for
humanitarian feelings by rescuing a young girl who was being dragged
to the police station on suspicion of prostitution. Garšin appeared
as a witness at the trial, and while admitting that the police had to
perform their duties, he put the blame for the girl's arrest solidly on
society. From Jakov Abramov, one of his earliest Russian bio-
graphers, comes a more bizarre anecdote: "He was involved there
[in Moscow] in a series of strange and absurd actions. For some
reason he wanted to see Kozlov who was then Chief of Police and he
attained his object in a rather peculiar way: he visited a brothel late
at night and began to stand drinks for all the girls; then, having run
up a rather high bill he refused to pay ... En route to the police
station, he threw away the twenty-five rubles he was carrying. Once
in the stationhouse he demanded an interview with Kozlov and
succeeded in talking to him." [38]

Garšin's two relevant stories, "An Incident" and "Nadejda
Nicolaievna," are clearly in the tradition of the fallen woman, with
their timid, virginal males and their proud, idealized women.
Although Nikitin in "An Incident" commits suicide in despair of
reforming the haughty and unrepentant Nadežda Nikolaevna, his
counterpart, the artist Lopatin, succeeds. Through his efforts, the
fallen woman is spiritually reborn, as even his rival is forced to
admit: "I only see that it is impossible to recognize this woman. I
know for certain that she has abandoned her former mode of life.
She has gone to some little room into which she does not allow
either Helfresch or her rescuer to enter. She sits for him, and, in
addition, does sewing." [39]

The reference to sewing is a characteristic cliché in the literary
treatment of the theme. Černyševskij's Krjukova works as a seamstress after her regeneration. Gogol''s Piskarev dreams that when

38. Jakov Abramov, *Vsevolod Mixajlovič Garšin* (St. Petersburg, 1889), p. 33.
39. Garshin, "Nadejda Nicolaievna," p. 209.

the fallen woman becomes his wife, she will sit beside him "sewing." The heroine of Nadson's "Slezy" remembers the innocent days when she was a "pure and timid blue-eyed seamstress." Tolstoj's Maslova sews before her seduction; afterwards she despises such "virtuous" employment. Finally, Čexov's Vasil'ev in "An Attack of Nerves" (1888) speaks of the "inevitable sewing machine" as a kind of stage prop for all rehabilitated prostitutes.

In the light of the literary as well as the biographical evidence surrounding Garšin, it is scarcely surprising that his name became associated with the problem of prostitution. When Čexov was asked to contribute to the memorial volume dedicated to Garšin's memory, he wrote to the poet Aleksej Pleščeev, one of the editors of the volume, that he had found an appropriate theme: "I have still another idea for a story: a young man with a character like Garšin's —a superior person, honorable and very sensitive—finds himself for the first time in his life in a house of prostitution.[40]

"An Attack of Nerves", the title under which the story finally appeared, is a tale of three young students who make a tour of the brothels in Moscow. One of them, Vasil'ev, is so shaken by the experience that he succumbs to a nervous collapse and requires medical treatment. Vasil'ev is obviously a literary projection of Garšin, for that author's qualities of compassion and sensitivity, prized in him by his contemporaries, are emphasized in Čexov's description:

> One of Vasilyev's friends had once said of him that he was a talented man. There are all sorts of talents—talent for writing, talent for the stage, talent for art; but he had a peculiar talent—a talent for *humanity*. He possessed an extraordinarily fine delicate scent for pain in general. As a good actor reflects in himself the movements and voice of others, so Vasilyev could reflect in his soul the sufferings of others. When he saw tears, he wept; beside a sick man, he felt sick himself and moaned; if he saw an act of violence, he felt as though he himself were the victim of it, he was frightened as a child, and in his fright ran to help. The pain of others worked on his nerves, excited him, roused him to a state of frenzy, and so on.[41]

40. A. P. Čexov, *Sočinenija* (Moscow: 1947), VII, 548.
41. Chekhov, "An Attack of Nerves," *The Portable Chekhov* (Viking: New York, 1947), p. 244.

Čexov skillfully contrasts Vasil'ev's romantically naïve and book-ish notions about fallen women with the reality of prostitution: "He knew nothing of fallen women except by hearsay and from books, and he had never in his life been to the houses in which they live . . . When it had happened to Vasilyev in the street to recognize a fallen woman by her dress or her manners, or to see a picture of one in a comic paper, he always remembered a story he had once read: a young man, pure and self-sacrificing, loves a fallen woman and asks her to become his wife; she, considering herself unworthy of such happiness, takes poison." [42]

The story that Vasil'ev had once read is, of course, Garšin's "An Incident"—only there the man rather than the woman commits suicide. Later in "An Attack of Nerves" Čexov describes a violinist whose "fresh youthful face" and talented playing seem out of place in the tawdry, stale atmosphere of the brothel, which is almost certainly an allusion to the romantic figure of the violinist in Garšin's "Nadejda Nicolaievna."

Čexov catches in a wonderfully delicate way all the faded, senti-mental notions that clung to the theme of the fallen woman:

> Vasilyev's imagination was picturing how, in another ten minutes, he and his friends would knock at a door; how by little dark passages and dark rooms they would steal in to the women; how, taking ad-vantage of the darkness, he would strike a match, would light up and see a martyred face and a guilty smile. The unknown, fair or dark, would certainly have her hair down and be wearing a white bed-jacket; she would be frightened by the light, would be fearfully confused, and would say: "For God's sake, what are you doing? Put it out!" It would all be dreadful, but interesting and novel. [43]

Whereas most writers on the theme tend to be somewhat heavy-handed in their descriptions of the brothel and prostitutes, Čexov preserves a lightness of touch. The reality of prostitution nevertheless turns out to be "prosaic, ordinary, uninteresting." A peculiar "tastelessness" characterizes it. Čexov describes the attendants at the brothel as both ordinary and sinister:

42. Chekhov, "An Attack of Nerves," pp. 222–223.
43. Chekhov, "An Attack of Nerves," p. 225.

Vasilyev took particular notice of the flunkeys in each house. In one of the houses—he thought it was the fourth—there was a little spare, frail-looking flunkey with a watch-chain on his waistcoat. He was reading a newspaper, and took no notice of them when they came in. Looking at his face Vasilyev, for some reason, thought that a man with such a face might steal, might murder, might bear false witness. But the face was really interesting: a big forehead, gray eyes, a little flattened nose, thin compressed lips, and a blankly stupid and at the same time insolent expression like that of a young harrier overtaking a hare. Vasilyev thought it would be well to touch this man's hair, to see whether it was soft or coarse. It must be coarse like a dog's.

The last sentence is a stroke of genius, but there are many other fine touches throughout the story: the newly fallen snow, the exhilaration of the night air, the romantic song of the students ("nevol'no k ètim grustnym beregam—menja vlečet nevedomaja sila"), Vasil'ev's "literary" reveries about fallen women. All these make a poignantly contrasting, gently ironic frame to the "poor and stupid" reality. It turns out that there are no "fallen women":

It seemed to him that he was seeing not fallen women, but things belonging to a different world quite apart, alien to him and incomprehensible; if he had seen this world before on the stage, or read of it in a book, he would not have believed it could exist . . .

There was much he did not understand about these houses, the souls of ruined women were a mystery to him as before; but it was clear to him that the situation was far worse than could have been believed. If that sinful woman who had poisoned herself was called fallen, it was difficult to find a fitting name for all these who were dancing now to this tangle of sound and uttering long, loathsome sentences. They were not on the road to ruin, but ruined.[44]

Vasil'ev, meanwhile, seriously considers all the possibilities of rehabilitating prostitutes. Čexov describes his notions on this subject in a passage that is at once a fine, perhaps unconscious imitation of Garšin's logical, classificatory style and a sympathetic insight into Garšin's personality:

It seemed to him that he must settle the question at once at all costs, and that this question was not one that did not concern him, but was his own personal problem . . . The method for attacking problems of all kinds was, as he was an educated man, well known to him. And

44. Chekhov, "An Attack of Nerves," pp. 229–230.

however excited he was, he strictly adhered to that method. He recalled the history of the problem and its literature, and for a quarter of an hour paced from one end of the room to the other trying to remember all the methods for saving women employed at the present time . . .

"All these not very numerous attempts," thought Vasilyev, "can be divided into three groups. Some, after buying the woman out of the brothel, took a room for her, bought her a sewing-machine, and she became a seamstress. And whether he wanted to or not, after having bought her out he made her his mistress; then when he had taken his degree, he went away and handed her into the keeping of some other decent man as though she were a thing. And the fallen woman remained a fallen woman. Others, after buying her out, took a lodging apart for her, bought the inevitable sewing-machine, and tried teaching her to read, preaching at her, and giving her books. The woman stayed and sewed as long as it was interesting and a novelty to her, then getting bored, began receiving men on the sly, or ran away and went back where she could sleep till three o'clock, drink coffee, and have good dinners. Finally, those who were most ardent and self-sacrificing took a bold, resolute step: they married the woman. And when the insolent and spoiled, or stupid and crushed animal became a wife, the head of a household, and afterwards a mother, it turned her whole existence and attitude to life upside down, so that it was hard to recognize the fallen woman afterwards in the wife and the mother. Yes, marriage was the best and perhaps the only means."

"But it is impossible!" Vasilyev said aloud, and he sank upon his bed. "I, to begin with, could not marry one! To do that one must be a saint and be unable to feel hatred or repulsion."

And even if one did marry a prostitute, what could one do about all the others, the new ones streaming in, the ten thousand in London, Hamburg? Poor Vasil'ev, who is thought to be mad because he worries about such problems, finally winds up in a psychiatrist's office. The story ends on an appropriate note of uncertainty:

> He had two prescriptions in his hand: one was for bromide, the other for morphine . . . He had taken all these remedies before!
> In the street he stood for a while and, saying good-by to his friends, dragged himself languidly to the university.[45]

Maxim Gor'kij's slight piece "Boles'" (1899) also concerns a fallen woman, who invents an imaginary lover (Boles') and asks a university student to write both his letters and her replies. The piece is

---

45. Chekhov, "An Attack of Nerves," pp. 242–243, 251.

partially redeemed from sentimentality by the economy and restraint of the narrative and by the liveliness of the prose. It ends on a
familiar humanitarian note: "The fallen classes, we say. And who
are the fallen classes, I should like to know? They are first of all
people with the same bones, flesh, blood and nerves as ourselves.
We have been told this day after day, for ages. And we actually
listen—and the devil only knows how hideous it all is. In reality,
we also are fallen people, and, so far as I can see, very deeply fallen
into the abyss of self-sufficiency and the conviction of our own
superiority." [46]

Literary conventions have a peculiar tenacity. Once established,
they die slowly and are constantly reborn. The literary convention of
the fallen woman, so prevalent in nineteenth-century Russian literature, did not die with that century. Kuprin's rather tedious novel of
prostitution, *Jama* (1909–1915), may be taken as a *summa* of the
fallen woman motif in Russian literature. Allusions appear in it to
stories on this theme by Čexov, Černyševskij, Krestovskij, and
Garšin, and it even includes an episode—complete with quotations
from Nekrasov's "When from thine error, dark, degrading"—dealing
with the rehabilitation of a fallen woman by an idealistic student.
The student at one point says that in this prostitute "perishes both a
splendid sister and a sainted mother," only to provoke from one of
his fellow-students the ironic query, "And will you buy her a sewing
machine?" [47] The students ultimately help their comrade to educate
the woman, who shows little talent for sewing but at least learns to
make artificial flowers. The student grows bored with her love, however, and manages to free himself from a liaison that has become
cloyingly domestic, leaving the woman to return to the brothel. It is
clear that even Kuprin's "realistic" picture of prostitution is
saturated with the literary tradition of the "fallen woman."

46. M. Gorkij, *Sobranie sočinenij* (Moscow, 1958), V, 165–166.
47. A. I. Kuprin, *Yama* (New York: The Modern Library, 1932), pp. 226–227.

THE POETRY OF GEORGIJ IVANOV

Irina Agushi

On August 26, 1958, a remarkable poet of the Russian emigration, Georgij Vladimirovič Ivanov, died in an old people's home in the south of France.[1] His death left one less witness to the Silver Age of Russian literature. The whirlwind of the Revolution had scattered the brilliant literary youth surrounding Blok and Gumilëv, and most of them had perished. Ivanov wrote of those masters in his reminiscences: "I've listened to their newly composed verses, drunk tea with them, strolled together with them along the streets of St. Petersburg ... However incomplete my notes about them, there remain perhaps only two or three persons in Russia who knew the poets as closely as I did, and abroad there is none."[2]

Georgij Ivanov is outstanding for his mastery of the technical side of prosody and for the elusive charm of his work. This elusiveness was already noticeable in the poet's early youth. While still a cadet, he liked to recite verses that were utterly incomprehensible to his fellow students. Nonchalantly he would utter a concatenation of sounds, such as:

> Стоны, звоны, перезвоны,
> Перезвоны, звоны, сны,
> Высоки крутые склоны,
> Крутосклоны зелены.

1. I wish to thank Gleb Struve for having indicated source materials, Vladimir Markov for providing transcripts of his private correspondence with Georgij Ivanov as well as valuable background information, and Jurij Ivask. Further, I should like to express my gratitude to the Russian émigré writers now living in France and England, particularly the poetess Irina Odoevzev, widow of Georgij Ivanov, and Jurij Terapiano, for their ready assistance and cooperation in permitting free access to private archives.
2. Georgij Ivanov, *Peterburgskie zimy* (New York: Chekhov, 1952), p. 200.

Then he would say with an enigmatic smile, burring his r's and lisping, "This is Sergej Gorodeckij," and one could not tell whether he admired the agglomeration of sonorous words or was merely laughing at them. "Žorž [as he was called] had a condescending, slightly contemptuous manner toward his interlocutor, a mixture between that of a lawyer and a high school pupil." It was hard to figure out his true attitude upon any subject. "Žorž Ivanov is a cadet just like any of us, coming from the same middle class officer background ... But he stands somewhat apart, he is little interested in our petty or large-scale 'collisions' with the school authorities, in football or the eternal single combats, which invariably begin with: —Now then, you sausage, come out into the open! ... At all this he looks with a kind of aesthetic snobbery that inspires respect even from the 'leaders' (carily) and the 'giants' (verzily).[3] Ivanov retained this characteristic even during his years of exile. By standing apart from the numerous self-important émigré organizations and refusing to participate in any of them, Ivanov incurred an ill will that caused constant unpleasantness for him and his wife. Indeed, Ivanov's aloofness was in part responsible for his untimely death.[4] He considered it demeaning to complain of his illness and delayed making the necessary official applications for a place in one of the rest homes in southern France.

Not much is known about the family of Georgij Ivanov. He seemed reluctant to talk about himself. When asked, he would dismiss the question with a jest. "I was greatly amused," he writes to a friend, "by your request to tell you more about my *papa* and *mama* for a future book on me, a posthumous one, I presume. If you wish to know who my *papa-mama* were, I shall answer you by quotations—first from Lermontov: 'ordinary Russian nobles,' and then from Stendhal: 'life smiled on them, and therefore they were not malicious.' This family trait stayed with me, too, although life has long since ceased to smile upon me."[5]

Ivanov was born in the province of Kovno on October 29, 1894. His father, an artillery officer in the guards, died when Žorž was ten.

3. Aleksandr Perfil'ev, "Georgij Ivanov," *Novoe russkoe slovo*, September 21, 1958.

4. Evgenij Jakonovskij, "G. Ivanov," *Russkaja mysl'*, August 29, 1959.

5. Ivanov to Vladimir Markov, June 22, 1956.

Soon after his father's death he entered the Cadet Corps in St. Petersburg. There he began to show an interest in literature, especially poetry. He joined the Ego-futurists, dedicating his first poem to Igor' Severjanin and Graal'-Arel'skij. The infatuation did not last long. In 1913 *Apollon*, an avant-garde literary journal of the time, printed an open letter by Ivanov, declaring his withdrawal from the literary circle "Ego" as well as his "complete nonparticipation in the scandalous and discreditable activity of the Glašataj and Nižegorodec publishing houses."[6]

Cadet Ivanov tried his hand at a number of poems, which appeared in 1912 under the title *Otplyt'e na ostrov Citeru* (Departure for the Island of Cythera). "*Citera* was written entirely at the school desk of 'His Majesty's Squad,' i.e., in the sixth and seventh forms of the Corps. A month after I sent this book to the editors of *Apollon*, I was awarded the title of 'member of the Cex.' Soon there appeared very flattering notices by Gumilёv in *Apollon* and Brjusov in *Russkaja mysl'*. Thus I dived, easily and effortlessly, into the very thick of literature, although I was disgustingly snobbish and silly."[7]

Ivanov graduated from the Cadet Corps and served for some time as an officer in the army, yet this activity was of so little importance to him that he left no records or details. It was literature that concerned him. From 1913 on, he contributed to *Apollon* both as poet and critic, and by 1922 he had published five more books of verse: *Gornica* (The Chamber, 1914), *Pamjatnik slavy* (Monument of Glory, 1915),[8] *Veresk* (Heather, 1916), *Sady* (Gardens, 1921), and *Lampada* (The Icon Lamp, 1922). Yet he was not really to find himself as a poet until after his exile. In 1921 he married the gifted poetess Irina Odoevceva, and the next year they emigrated through Riga and Berlin to Paris. There, together with Vladimir Xodasevič and Georgij Adamovič, Ivanov became a prominent figure in the Russian literary world.

From the late twenties until 1940, one of the customary social centers for émigré Russian writers was the apartment of Dimitrij

6. Georgij Ivanov, "Pis'ma v redakciju," *Apollon*, 6:91 (1913).
7. Ivanov to Markov, May 1, 1957. The Cex was the famous Cex poètov (Poet's Guild), headed by Gumilёv and including such poets as Anna Axmatova and Osip Mandel'štam.
8. This book was inaccessible to me when I was preparing this study.

Merežkovskij in Passy. Every Sunday the literary elite flocked in, drawn by Zinaida Gippius, Merežkovskij's spirited and sharp-tongued wife. Ivanov and Odoevceva regularly attended, along with such visitors as Adamovič, Mark Aldanov, Ivan Bunin, Nikolaj Berdjaev, Boris Vyšeslavcev, Vladimir Vejdle, Boris Zajcev, Konstantin Močul'skij, Sergej Makovskij, Nikolaj Ocup, Teffi, and Xodasevič. To create what they called an "incubator of ideas," the Merežkovskijs organized the Green Lamp Talks (Besedy zelenoj lampy). The chairman at these lively sessions was usually Georgij Ivanov.

The first major achievement of Ivanov's life in exile was a sixty-page volume of collected poems entitled *Rozy* (Roses), published in 1931. In this frightening book the poet portrays with unsparing clarity his concept of a Russian emigrant's fate and the tragic helplessness of the individual, who is being crushed, humiliated, and "bespattered with mud" by the Age of Mechanization. Ivanov further widened and intensified this theme in his three subsequent volumes of poetry: *Otplytie na ostrov Citeru* (Departure for the Island of Cythera, 1937), *Portret bez sxodstva* (A Portrait Without Resemblance, 1950), and *Dnevnik* (Diary, 1958). The complete and irreparable break of all ties with his homeland was one of the most difficult burdens of exile. As V. Mamčenko put it in a conversation with me, "Ivanov was thrust by reality into a state of insensibility," which in part limited his creative horizon and forced him to concentrate almost exclusively on the theme of death.

Ivanov never had a regular job, and his earnings from his writings were meager. Financial difficulties finally compelled the Ivanovs to move from Paris to a home for elderly Russian émigrés in Hyères. Such homes are usually melting pots of the most diverse professions and backgrounds, which rarely makes them compatible for persons whose interests lie above the commonplace. Georgij Ivanov had no one with whom to talk. Deprived of the life-giving stimulus offered by Paris, the cultural center, his health began to wane. He repeatedly requested transferral to a home near the capital. In a letter of February 1957 to the chairman of the Russian Émigrés Relief Committee, he asked, with a certain bitterness, why his "turn" seemed always to recede instead of approaching, notwithstanding his doctor's orders to leave the hot southern climate immediately because of his high blood pressure. "Doesn't even the title of The Top Émigré Poet, as I am being celebrated in print, give me the right to go to the head of the line for once?" But no argument could shake the adamant bureaucracy. He was destined to die in great pain while awaiting his "turn" in the "God-forsaken, abominable Hyères," as he used to call his dwelling place.

However, even if Ivanov the man could not escape the trials of life in exile, Ivanov the artist succeeded in transforming them into poetry and made of his agony a lasting song. After his death the journal *Novyj žurnal* began to print his unpublished poems under the heading *The Posthumous Diary*. Private archives in Paris still contain several dozens of his unpublished poems, which, it is hoped, will eventually find their way into Russian literary periodicals abroad. Most Russian writers now living in France agree that Ivanov's poetical talent was great. Such sweeping praise is rare in view of the number of literary factions that existed among Russian émigrés during his lifetime, and the ardor with which they fought each other.

THE "PARISIAN NOTE"

During the late twenties and early thirties the foreign literary life in Paris centered in Montparnasse. The Russians favored the café La Rotonde, whose owner, fancying himself as a poet, would serve coffee and onion soup on credit. In many cafés the price of a cup of coffee included free access to a large supply of hard-boiled eggs as well as the right to sit for as long as one liked, indoors or out. During the day the Russian writers had to toil for a living, doing manual work or driving taxis, for instance. But in the evening, especially on Thursdays and Saturdays, the tedium of existence was forgotten, and the gray, impersonal workers changed into literary personalities, independent and free: "Proust, André Gide, Joyce, Kafka, Gogol', Dostoevskij, Tolstoj, Rozanov, K. Leont'ev were constant topics of arguments and discussions. Everything incited a lively exchange of views: new books by Russian, French, German, English, and Italian authors, articles in journals, verses of the most varied poets. One talked about attitudes to art, to some poet's work; one analyzed past literary trends, both Russian and foreign, contemporary trends —and especially one verified one's own attitude, seeking new paths, thrusting aside whatever was false, any 'pose,' bombastic words, literary affectation (literaturnost').[9]

Within a few years a new *Weltanschauung* was gradually worked out in Montparnasse. Boris Poplavskij called it the "Parisian note" (parižskaja nota), and his term became an identifying label for the group who shared this point of view. Typical representatives were Poplavskij himself, Odoevceva, Vladimir Smolenskij, Nikolaj Ocup, Anatolij Šteiger, Lidija Červinskaja, and Antonin Ladinskij. The tone itself was set by Georgij Adamovič and Georgij Ivanov. Adamovič was influential chiefly in the field of literary criticism, as the principal critic of the newspaper *Poslednie novosti* and a constant collaborator in the journal *Sovremennye zapiski*. Ivanov's influence operated through his poetry, especially after the publication of *Rozy* in 1931. He in fact defined the Parisian Note as "a footnote to my poetry ... You see how presumptuous and how immodest I am." [10]

A number of factors contributed to the unique atmosphere that united this group of poets whose talents were so different. Although Goergij Fedotov argues against the existence of an actual Parisian school of Russian writers, one cannot overlook the fact that these writers shared certain characteristics.[11] Loss of homeland, exile, the void created in their souls from having lived through "Russia's fearful years," the impossibility of forgetting the past, the consciousness that their present emptiness could never be filled by mere words or beautiful imagery—these were the sources of their new poetic approach. Common to most was a refusal to accept oversimplified intellectual definitions, an aversion to rhetoric and insincerity, and a horror of literary imposture and philosophical speculation. Honesty was the principal feature of the Parisian Note.[12] The writings shared a dullness of color, muteness in sound, and restraint. Primness, oratory, and familiarity were unacceptable. Adamovič recalled: "We were nauseated by embellishments in poetry. We felt like running away from those flaunting *endimanché* verses. We were both amused and angered to read certain verbal fireworks with vertiginous rhymes, prodigious metaphors, and childish and barbarous inspiration un-

9. Jurij Terapiano, *Vstreči* (New York, 1953), pp. 96–97.
10. Ivanov to Markov (undated). Ivanov frequently failed to date letters.
11. Georgij Fedotov, "O Parižskoj poèzii," *Kovčeg* (New York, 1942), p. 189.
12. See Terapiano, *Vstreči*, pp. 148–154.

furled like a peacock's tail."[13] As Ivanov explained, "Poetry tries to make its essence inversely proportional to its impersonation in meter and imagery."[14] The usual form of poems was compressed, covering only twelve to sixteen lines.

A common subject was the condition of contemporary man, his inner self and his attitude to life.[15] The theme of "the man of the thirties" acquired a new and strictly personal feeling for these poets, who viewed man in a completely different light from that of their predecessors. They found themselves on the boundary between two epochs, their lost past and the unknowable future, forced to live in the empty interval separating these hostile worlds. Deprived of the old harmonies, they were as yet unable to accept the dissonant new universe. "The transition is slow and painful. The soul is frightened ... The night mist has fallen on the hills of Georgia—I should like to talk with life in words approximately like this ... but my soul mumbles some kind of 'dyr bu ščyl ubeščur.' It cannot keep silent, but it has forgotten how to speak ... Man, a little man, a zero looks ahead in perplexity. He sees a black void, and in it, like a flash of lightning, the incomprehensible substance of life."[16] What formerly would have been taken for "spiritual matter" was now seen as merely an irresponsible play with capitalized words. The poets of the Note came to hate easy answers to the "cursed questions," especially the rhetoric of metaphysics. Having lost their ability to accept half-answers, but at the same time finding no true answers, they were forced to remain alone in the cul-de-sac of their inner life.

The émigré poet had nowhere to turn for support: "The reading public is all of one color—it is tinged with indifferent weariness, and weariness (ustalost') rhymes with backwardness (otstalost') not just outwardly ... Everything that rises into the domain of the spiritual, religious, social quest (quest, and not established norms), into the realm of TRUE Russian culture, is being condemned as noxious, useless decadent writing."[17] Adamovič echoed Ivanov's complaints: "Life is hard for an émigré, because society does not exist and cannot

13. Georgij Adamovič, "Poèzija v èmigracii," *Opyty*, 4:56 (1955).
14. Ivanov, "Boris Poplavskij," *Čisla*, 5:231 (1931).
15. See Zinaida Gippius, "Čerty ljubvi," *Krug*, 3:139 (1938).
16. Ivanov, *Raspad atoma* (Paris, 1938), pp. 43–60.
17. Ivanov, "Bez čitatelja," *Čisla*, 5:151 (1941).

exist. There is only the appearance, a mirage, a kind of whipped-up foam on the surface of our relations, underneath which one is supposed to find living water . . . There is no place to escape to from oneself." [18]

With all other doors shut, their one outlet became art. This state of mind led to a feeling of nonbelonging (bespočvennost'), of irresponsibility, and of limitless creative freedom.

> И нет ни России, ни мира
> И нет ни любви, ни обид —
> По синему царству эфира
> Свободное сердце летит.
>
> (*R*, 30)[19]

Fedotov described the poet's situation: "One is given absolute, unheard-of freedom in emigration . . . No social obligations: let us investigate the subconscious mazes to the very bottom. No ethics: good and evil may both be used as means for a creative experiment. No dogmas: everything should be discovered anew. Perhaps there is even nothing to look for, perhaps all one has to do is simply to walk and describe that which can hardly be distinguished in the gloom." [20] These characteristics were of course not fostered solely by émigré life. They also bore the distinct mark of Innokentij Annenskij, whose name and literary influence had been handed down as a legacy by Adamovič and his disciples.[21]

18. Georgij Adamovič, "O literature v èmigracii," *Sovremmennye zapiski*, 58:452 (1935).

19. Citations of Ivanov's poems are indicated as follows. A page number alone refers to the collection *Stixi 1943–1958*. Otherwise the volume is noted in abbreviated form, followed by the page reference. *G—Gornica, L—Lampada, O.—Otplytie na ostrov Citeru* (1937), *O.* 1912—*Otplyt'e na ostrov Citeru* (1912), *P—Portret bez sxodstva, R—Rozy, S—Sady* (second edition), *V—Veresk* (second edition). For details of publication see Bibliography.

20. Fedotov, *Kovčeg*, p. 189.

21. "Creative power is amoral. Only when it 'adapts' itself to educational or ethical aims is it guided by categories alien to its nature. I think that for the sake of a full development of a person's spiritual life, one should not be unduly afraid, in poetry, of the feeling that beauty be victorious over the sense of duty." Innokentij Annenskij, *Kniga otraženij* (St. Petersburg, 1906), pp. 197–198. Cf. Ivanov:

Closely linked to the theme of person or self in the émigré poetry was an attempt to formulate one's elusive subconscious dreams. The poetical narrative became "jolted," marked by parentheses, series of dots, repetitions, and other devices of "subjectless muttering."[22] This style, however, was not characteristic of Ivanov. In this respect he stood apart from the rest of the group. In *Rozy*, and later in *Portret* and *Dnevnik*, each word was weighty, for each sprang from one dominant thought and aimed toward its inevitable conclusion. Conciseness, precision, and simplicity, in fact, earned Ivanov the appellation "master of form." At the same time his attitude toward form showed a contradiction. The Parisian Note, mainly through its mouthpiece Adamovič, preached a contempt for form. This view led to bitter polemics between him and Xodasevič, who maintained that one should first learn the technique of prosody. Ivanov seemed to support the thesis of Adamovič. He even wrote: "verse can be paeonic, pyrrhic, etc. One may, of course, evaluate and analyze it from this angle; but, on the whole, it is a boring occupation . . . One could similarly analyze and define the chemical composition of spring air, yet how much more natural and easy it is just to take a deep breath of it."[23]

According to Irina Odoevceva, verse writing came easily to Ivanov. He often jotted down poems in cafés, trains, or wherever he happened to be in the hustle and bustle of the great city. He never toiled over lines. It seems that "Otzovis' kukušečka," for instance, was written in a few minutes, while waiting for a train. When I went

---

21. [*cont.*]   Игра судьбы. Игра добра и зла.
             Игра ума. Игра воображенья.
             "Друг друга отражают зеркала,
             Взаимно искажая отраженья"...

                          (22)

             Она прекрасна, эта мгла,
             Она похожа на сиянье.
             Добра и зла, добра и зла
             В ней неразрывное слиянье.

                        (*O*, 17)

22. See Ivanov, "Sinevatoe oblako," *R*, 47.

23. Ivanov, "Literatura i žizn'," *Vozroždenie*, 8:198 (1950). See also 6:119 (1949): "A Russian writer never was, and I hope, never will be a cold aesthete, an indifferent 'appraiser of the beautiful,' showing little interest in the personality of the poet."

through some of Georgij Ivanov's manuscripts in 1960, I came across small pieces of note paper on which were written such technically perfect poems as "Otvlečennoj složnost'ju persidskogo kovra" (*Dnevnik*), "Grustno, drug" (*Rozy*), and "Tak il' ètak" (*Otplytie*, 1937). Petr Bicilli calls this last poem "one of the most successful."[24] Thus, although Ivanov ostensibly had a disdain for form, he clearly possessed a perfect mastery of verse technique. On looking deeper into his poetry, however, one is also inclined to agree with Gumilëv that "the conscious often likes to deck itself with the unconscious."[25]

Georgij Ivanov was the only poet of the Parisian Note to succeed in convincing the reader that "Nothing IS." This persuasiveness was the result of conscious creative art. "Poetry is artful prose," Ivanov said once (79). It was a mistake for the Paris poets to rest their new poetry of negation exclusively on the humane note, discarding any concern with how this humane element could be better expressed in poetic form. They forgot what Xodasevič had once remarked: "The too human is often untragic in tragedy and unpoetic in poetry."[26]

LITERARY LEGACIES AND AFFINITIES

Georgij Ivanov's poetry is full of quotations, allusions, and deliberate poetical echoes. It is not my intention to discuss the literary influences on him, but rather to cite a series of parallels illustrating certain literary legacies and affinities, in hopes of highlighting the most characteristic features of Ivanov's work and offering a better insight into his artistic personality.

His early descriptive period, for instance, typified by a minute attention to detail, stands out more clearly when projected against the refined, studied elegance of the poetry of Mixail Kuzmin (1875–1935), who brought to life "the spirit of trifles, light and charming." Compare, for instance, an early poem by Ivanov:

> Кофейник, сахарница, блюдца,
> Пять чашек с узкою каймой

24. Petr Bicilli, "Georgij Ivanov," *Sovremennye zapiski*, 64:459 (1937).
25. Nikolaj Gumilev, "Žizn' stixa," *Apollon*, 7:9 (1910).
26. Vladislav Xodasevič, "V. Ropšin. Kniga stixov," *Sovremennye zapiski*, 49:448 (1932).

> На голубом подносе жмутся,
> И внятен их рассказ немой.
>
> (*V*, 16)

with Kuzmin's "china poetry":

> Сквозь чайный пар я вижу гору Фузий
> На желтом небе золотой вулкан.
> Как блюдечко природу странно узит!
> Но новый трепет мелкой рябью дан.
>
> ("Фузий в блюдечке")

A whole period of Ivanov's creative process is here made clearer. It can best be expressed by Kuzmin's own words: "How strangely a saucer narrows nature."

Another affinity, on quite a different plane, exists between the two poets: their refraction of reality through the fantastic. Kuzmin populates his poetic world from time to time with harlequins, columbines, and jugglers, who hide their true selves behind a distorting mask. "Those—are not us."[27] The theme of the mask, with its appalling unreality, was also developed by Ivanov into a literary device, as in:

> Маскарад был давно, давно окончен,
> Но в тайном зале маски бродили,
> Только их платья стали тоньше:
> Точно из дыма, точно из пыли.
>
> (*G*, 58)

However, the poets differ in their interpretation of this theme. With Kuzmin, one discerns behind the mask the familiar human image, whereas Ivanov's buffoon transforms everything into an ominous instability: "He sways by his sighs love, mirth, and snug security" (*G*, 23). The texture of what appears to be ordinary and reliable is cut open, and from the void appear ghost-masks. They impart a dread of the unknown, which shocks even more when presenting itself in a buffoonish disguise, as in Ivanov's "Figljar" (*G*, 25). To only a few, such as Pierrot or the buffoon, is the ability

27. Kuzmin, *Seti*, p. 19.

given to see through the opening in the web "the claws of sunset" (*G*, 13), and they try to conceal the fateful impress of this knowledge on their faces behind a facetious make-up. Ivanov's two-faced Pierrot is at once a jester and a tragedian:

> Я кривляюсь вечером на эстраде:
> Пьеро двойник.
> А после, ночью, в растрепанной тетради
> Веду дневник.
>
> (*G*, 27)

Ivanov would wholeheartedly subscribe to Kuzmin's uttering: "Fate does not put a full stop at the end, but only a blot." [28]

Despite the fact that Ivanov began his literary career as a member of the Poet's Guild, its most outspoken representative, Nikolaj Gumilëv, exercised only a limited influence on him. Indeed, Gumilëv's legacy was confined solely to the technical side of their craft. Ivanov himself later admitted that he had loved everything that Gumilëv could not stand.

Gumilëv's evaluation of young Ivanov's verses was restricted by the range of his own poetic vision. In his survey of *Gornica*, Gumilëv noted Ivanov's contemplative instinct, his "flaneur psychology," and his mastery of speech, yet such poems as "Ja pomnju svody nizkogo podvala" (*G*, 30) or "Kitajskie drakony nad Nevoj" (*G*, 21) remained outside his scope. He merely saw in them "a good deal of naïve romanticism" and called their author "adept at interesting adventure poetry." [29] In discussing a second collection by the young poet, *Veresk*, Gumilëv again commended his visual perception of the world, exhibited in descriptive details. He admitted Ivanov's skill in verse composition, yet regretted that *Veresk* did not contain those "previous nice and simple little songs." He rebuked the poet for his unsuccessful imitation of Kuzmin's love poems, and even questioned if Ivanov would be able and willing "to think seriously whether or not he should become a poet, that is, someone who is always going ahead." [30]

28. Kuzmin, Epilog, *Seti*, p. 44.
29. Nikolaj Gumilev, "Pis'mo o russkoj poèzii," *Apollon*, 5:39 (1914).
30. Gumilev, *Apollon*, 1:28 (1916).

Though he lacked understanding in matters alien to his nature, Gumilëv was a good judge of the poet's craft. He bequeathed to his disciples the minute concern of a poet-craftsman to polish and chisel his verse; an awareness of the importance of every word; and a desire to forge syllables into new shapes. Gumilëv dedicated his entire life to one goal: instilling in others an awareness of what St. John had proclaimed in the Gospel, namely, that "The Word was God."[31]

The significance of Ivanov as a poet is based on his mastery over words, on "the triumph of the most common words that sing precisely in this combination and in no other."[32] His poems offer many instances of lexical fullness of meaning. In the following lines, for example, the additional prefix *pri-* with *podnimaetsja* harbors the possibility of some unexpected action, being also supported by the epithets "disquieting," "pale," and "restless":

> И над тревожными волнами
> В воздухе гаснущем, бледна,
> За беспокойными ветвями
> Приподнимается луна.
>
> (*V*, 43)

The words used by Ivanov are ordinary words; they do not strike the reader if taken out of context. It is only in their inter-relation with other, similar, plain words that they acquire a new power and significance.

Hardly a poet at the beginning of the twentieth century remained immune to Blok's influence, and Ivanov was no exception. Blok's theme of "unreal reality," of perceiving life as a dream in its monotonous repetition of the familiar cycle ("Noč', ulica, fonar', apteka") reverberates in *Rozy*:

> Сто лет вперед, сто лет назад,
> А в мире все одно —
> Собаки лают, да глядят
> Мечтатели в окно.
>
> (*R*, 44)

---

31. Ivanov, "O Gumileve," *Sovremennye zapiski*, 47:306 (1931).
32. Nikolaj Ocup, "Pamjati Georgija Ivanova," *Russkaja mysl'*, September 9, 1958.

But while Blok created a mystical reality for himself, Ivanov remained aloof from metaphysical speculation. Blok seems to have been disturbed that Ivanov could launch himself into a world of creative phantasy spontaneously, without any artificial springboard —whether philosophical, metaphysical, or religious: "Whenever I begin to read poems by G. Ivanov, I unfailingly meet with good, almost flawless verses, written with intelligence and taste, with a great cultural understanding and tact; there is nothing trivial, nothing vulgar in them. At first you begin to get angry at such perfection, because you cannot make out where these verses come from or what they are about. But this feeling is suppressed by the indubitable talent of the author . . . Listening to such verse as is collected in the book *Gornica*, one can start weeping, not about the verses or their author, but about our impotence and the fact that there can exist such frightening lines about nothing. These poems possess everything, and yet one cannot do anything with it." [33] Proceeding from a completely different concept of poetry for its own sake,[34] Ivanov nevertheless showed considerable influence of Blok. Even *Rozy*, in which Ivanov finally found himself, "stood under the sign of Blok." [35]

An element of lyrical melodiousness permeates the texture of Ivanov's poetry. For him, as for Blok, music was a reality. Blok divided time and space into two spheres: historical, "calendar time," and "noncalendar," musical time. In order to live in the second sphere, one must achieve a bodily and spiritual balance; should this be lost, musical hearing is also lost.[36] Blok's creative process was closely linked with his internal rhythm, and the loss of his hearing in 1918 led to the poet's creative death.

Music was likewise a constant inspiration to Ivanov, even though he occasionally said, "I do not need music any longer." His attitude was dual. At times, music appears in his poetry as a symbol of "hope, life, and freedom" (*O*, 20) and is associated with light: "the white

33. Aleksandr Blok, *Očerki, stat'i i reči* (Moscow, 1955), pp. 300–302.

34. Jurij Terapiano, "Georgij Ivanov: 1943–1958 Stixi," *Russkaja mysl'*, November 8, 1958.

35. Gleb Struve, *Russkaja literatura v izgnanii* (New York: Chekhov, 1956), p. 321.

36. Aleksandr Blok, "Krušenie gumanizma," *Sočinenija v dvux tomax* (Moscow: Gosudarstvennoe izdatel'stvo xudožestvennoj literatury, 1955), II, 313–314.

wing of music"; "music illumines the path" (*Čisla*, 1930, bk. 4, p. 7); "music alone does not deceive" (*O*, 19). At other times, the poet views music as a dark force of "sorcery" (*R*, 35), a "delirium" (*Sovr. zap.* 50:327, 1932), and he links it with gloom:

> Пусть себе, как черная стена,
> К звездам поднимается она,
> Пусть себе, как черная волна,
> Глухо рассыпается она.
>
> (*O*, 14)

"The characteristic ternary meter of Blok presents a perfect analogy to the waltz."[37] This is exactly how Ivanov apprehended the rhythmic expression of Blok's "music":

> Это черная музыка Блока
> На сияющий падает снег
>
> (*O*, 27)

and he often submitted to the hypnotic incantation of its rhythm, as in:

> Ласково кружимся в вальсе загробном
> На эмигрантском балу.
>
> (47)

The core of Ivanov's perception of the world comes to light when comparing his use of imagery with Blok's. To Blok, sunsets are heavenly gates into eternity; they speak, promise, remind, tempt, beckon. To Ivanov, the sunset usually represents a breach into a "resonant void."[38] The impressive vessels of Blok, which figure as

37. Petr Bicilli, "Pljaska smerti," *Vstreči*, 4:172–176 (1934).
38. Compare:

> Ты в поля отошла без возврата,
> Да святится имя Твое!
> Снова красные копья заката
> Протянули ко мне острие.
>
> (Blok, I, 138)

symbols of hope, become in Ivanov light craft, sailboats, small yawls—aerial and almost transparent images in the style of Antoine Watteau.[39]

Another image central to both is snow. It imparts movement to Blok's lines, assuming the shape of a snowstorm that upheaves, drifts, sweeps, sways, and runs; one can almost hear the whistling and howling of the wind. "*The Snow Mask* is not a collection of poems about the snow, it is the snowstorm itself."[40] With Ivanov one enters into a silent and motionless world, entirely covered with ice, the silence broken only by "sighs of the abyss." Phantoms move along the ice (*O*, 68). This world is "utterly frozen and, eternally hopeless" (*O*, 42), but at the same time extremely fragile, as if placed on "the tenuous spring ice" (*O*, 46). A tiny melting ice-floe being carried away to the south embodies all human happiness (*O*, 64, 67).

Both poets also regarded art as hell. According to Blok, the "lilac worlds had engulfed Lermontov and Gogol', for art is a monstrous and glittering inferno. Out of its darkness the artist invokes his images."[41] "Art is nothing but a luminous hell," asserts Ivanov. He liked to dwell and grieve alone in his orange-colored Hades. He was not interested in people, nor did he even seem to notice them. His highly personal poetry concentrates on the poet's inner self, his feelings, moods, and torments.

Ivanov's muse was the result of blissful inspiration and oppressive incarnation. The poet tried to arrest his vision of the beautiful by means of words.[42] But he often felt that words fell short of their task of recreating the momentary vision, and that he, as a poet, had failed in his attempt to reunite the broken pieces of the ideal image perceived by him in a fleeting moment of inspiration. He was acutely aware of the inadequacy of his creative power.

Все безнадежней, все желтей
Пустое небо. Там у ската
На бледной коже след когтей
Отпламеневшего заката.
(*G*, 13)

39. E.g., Ivanov, "Legkie lodki," *R*, 49; "Parusa uplyvajut na sever," *O*, 23.
40. Kornej Čukovskij, *Aleksandr Blok* (Petrograd: A. F. Marks, 1924), p. 121.
41. Aleksandr Blok, "O sovremennom sostojanii russkogo simvolizma," *Apollon*, 8:27 (1910).
42. Compare Blok, "Xudožnik," I, 395.

Да, я еще живу. Но что мне в том,
Когда я больше не имею власти
Соединить в создании одном
Прекрасного разрозненные части.

(О, 38)

This torment of "unresolved polyphony" was also well known to Innokentij Annenskij. He was painfully aware that violin strings can only sing at the contact of the cutting bow. "What seemed to be music to the listeners, was torment for them."[43] The inevitability of pain and death is a predominant theme with both Annenskij and Ivanov. Their dual interpretations of this theme are remarkably similar: they emanate a kind of sad affection, and at the same time are quaintly interlaced with the jeering humor of the hangman.

Есть слова — их дыханье, что цвет,
Так же нежно и бело-тревожно,
Но меж них ни печальнее нет,
Ни нежнее тебя, *невозможно.*

(Annenskij)[44]

Этой жизни нелепость и нежность
Проходя, как под теплым дождем,
Знаем мы — впереди неизбежность,
Но ее появленья не ждем.

(56)

Meandering through the texture of this enchanting hopelessness, breaking up the melancholy evenness of the surface, is a sneering element:

И был бы мой бессмертный дух
Теперь не дух, он был бы Бог...
Когда-б не *пиль* да не *тубо,*
Да не *тю-тю* после *бо-бо!..*

(Annenskij)[45]

---

43. "I bylo mukoju dlja nix,/Čto ljudjam muzykoj kazalos'." Innokentij Annenskij, *Stixotvorenija i tragedii* (Leningrad: Bol'šaja biblioteka poèta, 1959), p. 100.

44. Annenskij, "Nevozmožno," *Stixotvorenija i tragedii,* p. 158.

45. Annenskij, "Čelovek," *Stixotvorenija i tragedii,* p. 146.

Уплывают маленькие ялики
В золотой междупланетный омут.
Вот уже растаял самый маленький,
А за ним и остальные тонут.

    На последней самой утлой лодочке
    Мы с тобой качаемся вдвоем:
    Припасли, дружок, немного водочки,
    Вот теперь ее и разопьем...

                             (67)

Both poets were attracted by the inexpressible sadness of evanescence:

Я люблю на бледнеющей шири
В переливах растаявший цвет...
Я люблю всё, чему в этом мире
Ни созвучья, ни отзвука нет.
                    (Annenskij)[46]

Я люблю безнадежный покой,
В октябре — хризантемы в цвету,
Огоньки за туманной рекой,
Догоревшей зари нищету...

    Тишину безымянных могил,
    Все банальности "Песен без слов,"
    То, что Анненский жадно любил,
    То, чего не терпел Гумилев.

                             (87)

Unlike Annenskij, however, who was always original in his expressions and metaphors, Ivanov seldom stepped beyond the limits of everyday words. He delighted in playing with them, making common, trivial words mock their own nature as well as the banality of life. One should not expect to hear through his lines "the peal of bells that go off to the blue hermitage of heaven to pray," nor to come upon "the stalks of meditation grown to a startling fairy-tale," nor to find "the paper of one's heart, crumpled by anguish." [47]

Both Annenskij and Ivanov visualized snow as a symbol of un-

46. Annenskij, "Ja ljublju," *Stixotvorenija i tragedii*, p. 147.
47. Annenskij, "Zakatnyj zvon v pole," p. 147; "Dal'nie ruki," p. 149; "Drugomu," p. 156.

marred beauty sacrificed to spring.[48] They loved the tenuous, thawing snow with a tender affection. The moment of transition appealed to their artistic perception; they liked to pause on the borderline of existence and to record the sensation of finding oneself standing on a blade of grass between a chasm and an abyss. Ivanov's muse, like that of Annenskij, also grew among "thorns" ("Na šipax ot muki povorota").[49] This torment of growth manifests itself in the intimate tone of Ivanov's poems. "In my opinion," remarks Roman Gul', "the whispering voice of Ivanov has only two predecessors in Russian literature: Rozanov in prose, and Annenskij in poetry. No one else in our literature was capable of speaking so softly, almost in one's ear, and at the same time of cutting one as if with a razor blade. Georgij Ivanov possessed the gift of such intimacy."[50]

"Take care of the intimate; the intimacy of your soul is more precious than all the treasures of the world," was Rozanov's advice. Rozanov created a new literary expression in the form of "thought fragments" in his *Uedinennoe* and *Opavšie list'ja*. He attained an intimate, antiliterary effect through colloquial stylization, the use of short, simple sentences, and by debunking the lofty and dignifying the lowly. In Ivanov's last work, a diary in verse, he chose similar antiliterary devices. A close parallel exists between the metaphor of "God who irons man with a heavy iron" in Rozanov's *Opavšie list'ja*[51] and the tailor-creator ironing a new suit and producing a new work of art in Ivanov's "Portnoj obnovočku utjužit" (42).

Besides such purely literary devices, the works of both Rozanov and Ivanov shared a similarity in their total absence of ethical inhibition. As Rozanov explained, "I don't even know whether one writes 'morality' (nravstvennost') with a '*ě*' or '*e*', nor do I know who its daddy and mummy were, and whether it had any children, and what its address is—I don't know anything at all about it."[52] Fedotov defined Ivanov's view thus: "Ivanov does not seek, he

---

48. Compare Annenskij, "Doč Iaira," and "Sneg," *Stixotvorenija i tragedii*, pp. 126–127, with Ivanov's "Gde prošlogodnij sneg" (23), quoted below.

49. Annenskij, "Staraja šarmanka," p. 102.

50. Roman Gul', Introduction to Ivanov, *Stixi 1943–1958*, p. 16.

51. Vasilij Rozanov, *Opavšie list'ja* (St. Petersburg, 1913), p. 105.

52. Rozanov, *Opavšie list'ja*, p. 189.

does not travel through ideals and souls. Evil for him is probably more attractive than good—at least esthetically."[53]

Similar words were once used of François Villon, whose voice reached the artistic ear of Ivanov. "I know Villon by heart," Ivanov wrote to a friend. "Mais où sont les neiges d'antan?" asks Villon, and across the span of centuries an echo is heard:

> Где прошлогодний снег, скажите мне?..
> Нетаявший, почти альпийский снег,
> Невинной жертвой отданный весне,
> Апрелем обращенный в плеск и бег,
> В дыханье одуванчиков и роз,
> Взволнованного мира светлый вал,
> В поэзию,
>   В бессмысленный вопрос,
> Что ей Виллон когда-то задавал?
>
>   (23)

Villon exposes the evil of death in his ballad "Les regrets de la Belle Heaulmière." The first part celebrates the transient beauty of youth; in the second part, its antithesis, age gradually disfigures the lovely features of Heaulmière, until they become a specter of decay. Villon fragmentizes the very perfection that he had earlier in the poem created, but the beauty of his artistic expression remains intact, triumphing over the laws of nature.[54] The poem would seem to prove that the chief purpose of Nature, as Oscar Wilde put it, is to illustrate quotations from the poets, just as the raison d'être of literature is to anticipate life. While some literary critics saw in Villon's verse the expression of his own wicked disposition, he was merely imitating the grotesque songs then prevalent in the north of France. The poetry of both Villon and Ivanov contains elements characteristic of this grotesque genre, such as dramatic confrontation, contrast, or images and scenes in motion. But while Villon's dramatic effects are limited to the opposition of "le povre Villon" and "Villon le bon follastre," Georgij Ivanov enlarges them to metaphysical proportions.

Villon paid special attention to the word as such. "He took care to say things as completely as possible with the fewest words pos-

---

53. Fedotov, *Kovčeg*, p. 189.
54. Compare Ivanov, "Ešče ja naxožu očarovan'e," *Stixi 1943–1958*, p. 62.

sible."[55] He used words in much the same way as did Ivanov, employing a vocabulary of everyday expressions—"verbal combinations"—which he transformed into sounds that "charm and confuse us."[56]

The *Little Testament* of Villon is full of that charmingly caustic irony by which one also recognizes the later Ivanov. It is written in the form of a diary, as is Ivanov's last volume of collected poems. This form influences, and was meant to influence, the reader's reactions, stirring up "intimate echoes" in his innermost self.

However, one should beware of falling into the trap set by a "confiding friend" to catch us unawares. The soft intimate whisper of Ivanov's *Dnevnik* reveals little of the intimate side of its author, but a great deal about his relation to art.

THE EARLY PERIOD, 1912–1923

The poetical activity of Georgij Ivanov began among the Ego-futurists. Following the example of the *maître* of this group, Igor' Severjanin, Ivanov called his first poems "poèzy." He was associated with poets like Konstantin Olimpov (*Aèroplannye poèzy*), Graal'-Arel'skij, I. Lukaš, and others who helped edit the *Almanac Ego*. Benedikt Livšic, in his book *Polutoraglazyj strelec*, evokes with good-natured humor the congenial atmosphere in which these brethren of the pen lived and wrote. Later, Georgij Ivanov referred to that period of his poetical beginnings thus: "A friend of the family entertained our guests by reading his 'decadent' verses. I was sixteen and I too was writing verses, also decadent ones, by the dozen."[57]

Otplyt'e na ostrov Citeru, published in 1912, was the eighteen-year-old poet's first attempt at versification. Bearing the dedication "to my best friend—sister Nataša with tender affection," the small volume has four main parts: I. The Love Mirror, II. The Keyboard

55. Louis Charpentier, *François Villon* (Paris, 1933), p. 63.
56. "Pourquoi en recevons-nous tantôt la simple impression plastique d'une combinaison verbale ... d'autre fois, pourquoi ces mots retentissent-ils en nous comme un chant qui nous charme ou nous trouble ou nous soulève et qui, éveillant en nous d'intimes échos, semble retentir au fond de nous-mêmes?" Maurice Allem, Introduction to François Villon, *Oeuvres complètes* (Paris, 1945), p. lii.
57. Georgij Ivanov, "O Gumileve," *Sovremennye zapiski*, 47:310 (1931).

6—H.S.S.

of Nature, III. When the Leaves Fall, and IV. God's Sun, as well as
a Prologue and an Epilogue.[58] In it the lyrical "I" is stylized. At
times the poems assume the mannerism of Severjanin, as in "Ja
dolgo ždal poslanija ot Vas"; occasionally they imitate Kuzmin or
echo a pseudo-religious meditative mood, as in "Solnce Božie" and
"Osennij brat":

> Он — инок. Он — Божий. И буквы устава
> Все мысли, все чувства, все сказки связали.
> В душе его травы, осенние травы,
> Печальные лики увядших азалий.
>
> (*O.* 1912, 24)

Sixteen of the thirty-six poems are written in free accentual verse
with ternary or binary bases. The ternary basis is obvious in "Zarja
pasxal'naja," "Solnce Božie," and particularly in "Ptica upala,"
which may even be considered as a transitional form from dactyl to
dol'nik.[59] A binary trochaic basis is evident in "Pesnja o pirate Ole,"
where twenty-nine out of thirty-six lines are trochaic.[60] Thematically

---

58. I. Любовное зеркало. II. Клавиши природы. III. Когда падают
листья. IV. Солнце Божие. At present the only copy of this volume in the
United States is in private hands.

59.   Господня грудь прободенная
                Точит воду и кровь,
                Учит верить в любовь
                Грудь, копием прободенная.
                            (*O.* 1912, 28)

                Заиграли лучи в киоте,
                Пробежали по древку креста,
                И зардели раны Христа...
                Вновь пылают глаза и уста
                У икон в запыленном киоте.
                            (*O.* 1912, 28)

60.   Кто отплыл ночью в море
                С грузом золота и жемчугов
                И стоит теперь на якоре
                У пустынных берегов?
                Это тот, кого несчастье
                Помянуть три раза вряд.
                Это Оле — властитель моря,
                Это Оле — пират.
                            (*O.* 1912, 18)

and rhythmically this ballad is reminiscent of Gumilëv.[61] One cannot find so high a percentage of rhythmic variations in Ivanov's mature work as in this first volume of verse. *Otplyt'e* also contains the "gazella" ("Skakal ja na svoem kone k tebe, o ljubov'") and four triolets ("Vljublenie," "Otvergnutaja strast'," "Sčastlivyj primer," and "Utešenie"). The volume may be regarded mainly as an exercise in the art of versification. Ivanov referred to these poems as "trinkets (stekljaški)."[62]

Despite their modest range of traditional thematics and lyric form, the poems in *Otplyt'e* show signs of the purely "Ivanovian" manner yet to come. Lifeless grass blades and faded azalias softly bend down to a background of pastoral songs (*O.* 1912, 24). Through the strains of the pipe one can detect a whisper from the empty heights of the void (*O.* 1912, 14), and the shepherd himself changes imperceptibly into a lifeless form (*O.* 1912, 16). Here and there, the vivid canvass becomes obscured by a shadow; the sun loses its brilliance, its red disk heralds darkness, which brings after it a moonlike world in which there is no longer any trace of mischievous cupids, a world woven of "smoke and dust" (*O.* 1912, 25). The lyrical reality of the moon world will eventually become the only reality for Ivanov, and the sun world become simply an object for poetic game. But for the time being, despite the gathering shadows, the sun continues to shine over *Otplyt'e*, and while the bold sailors depart "from autumn to spring," it promises them a bright harbor:

> Мы — в дерзкое стремимся плаванье
> И мы — смелее с каждым днем.
> Судьба ведет нас к светлой гавани,
> Где все горит иным огнем!
>
> (*O.* 1912, 31)

This spirited verse, full of hopes for a happy new day, closes the volume.

61. Compare Gumilev's poem "Vljublennaja v djavola," *Sobranie sočinenij*, I (Washington, 1962), 64.

62. Undated letter to Markov. The military verse of *Monument of Glory* (1915) may have been the same sort of exercise. Ivanov remarked only, in another undated letter: "I have a whole book, *Pamjatnik slavy*, in magnificent iambics— 'ura, ura, ura za russkogo carja!' And many, as for instance Brjusov, have praised it."

Ivanov's other three books of verse from this period—*Gornica* (1914), *Veresk* (1916), and *Lampada* (1922)—share a common development in compositional methods and certain elements of style. The blended meter of *Otplyt'e* gives way to varied rhyme combinations: the crossed rhyme of the heroic quatrain (abab), the couplet form (aabb), and the binding rhyme (abba) are now varied with single, double, polysyllabic, perfect, or approximate rhymes, with feminine, hypermetrical, and truncated endings. The majority of the rhyming words belong to heterogeneous grammatical categories: *myši–tiše, oborvut–ujut, pole–bole* (*G*, 23, 36).

However, with few exceptions, like the inexact rhyme *potëmkami–kómkaeš'* (*G*, 34), the rhyming pattern adheres to the accepted norm of the period. One cannot speak of innovations of any kind in Georgij Ivanov's poetic technique.[63] Different rhymes are used with moderation, just as meter modulations in *Otplyt'e* never went beyond the established norms of prosody. Ivanov tends to minimize irregularity; he avoids excess, emphasizing the importance of preserving a sense of proportion.

> И черни, требующей новизны,
> Он говорит: "Нет новизны. Есть мера."
> (86)

Vladimir Smolenskij, in his survey of *Portret bez sxodstva* (1950), mentions Ivanov's "sense of measure," and Petr Bicilli writes:

---

63. Sometimes, however, he does experiment. For example, he introduces the rather daring shift of stress in the trisyllabic key words "slušaet," "pleščetsja," and "vozduxe" in the following lines:

> Насторожившееся ухо
> Слушает медленный прибой:
> Плещется море мерно, глухо,
> Словно часов старинных бой.
>
> И над тревожными волнами
> В воздухе гаснущем, бледна,
> За беспокойными ветвями —
> Приподнимается луна.
> (*V*, 43)

"There is no showiness in Ivanov; each and all of his poems leave the impression of one whole, of ONE WORD."[64]

Veresk, the second book of this group, is much akin to *Gornica* in its formal structure and its descriptive style. "Georgij Ivanov's verses capture us by their concreteness," Gumilëv wrote about *Veresk*. "This book has a unifying purpose—the wish to perceive and to depict the world as a series of visual images."[65] Few can equal Ivanov's descriptive art, his ability to create a complete picture out of minute fragments of detail. Very successful examples are the poems "Kak xorošo i grustno vspominat'/O Flandrii neprixotlivom ljude," "Na starom dedovskom kisete," and "Ameriki oborvannaja karta" (*V*, 25, 27, 10).

The nature of these contemplative descriptions gradually changes from the purely visual observation of objects that suggest a certain period or place to the animation of the objects themselves:

> Китайские драконы над Невой
> Раскрыли пасти в ярости безвредной
> (*G*, 21)

The creative process leads further, to the reduction of organically living things to inanimate categories:

> О, празднество на берегу, в виду искусственного моря.
> (*V*, 13)

> Заря шафранная — в бассейне догорая —
> Дельфину золотит густую чешую
> И в бледных небесах искусственного рая
> Фонтана легкую, чуть слышную струю.
> (*V*, 35)

Such displacement of accepted concepts seems to cut away the ground from under one, but the uniform rhythm lulls the reader into accepting the new, unfamiliar poetic reality.

Smoothly flowing rhythmic phrases are heard much later, after Ivanov has fully developed his art of "contrast composition." But

64. Vladimir Smolenskij, "'Portret bez sxodstva' G. Ivanova," *Vozroždenie*, 32:140 (1954); Bicilli, "'Otplytie na ostrov Citeru Georgija Ivanova," *Sovremennye zapiski*, 64:459 (1937).
65. Gumilev, "Pis'mo o russkoj poèzii," *Apollon*, 1:27 (1916).

even in *Lampada*—perhaps the weakest of this group of three books —parallel constructions and internal rhymes, absent before, help to create a melodious quality in the verse. In sum, *Gornica, Veresk,* and *Lampada* contain the characteristic elements of Georgij Ivanov's early lyrics: a keen sense for descriptive detail; an impassive narrative style, expressed in smooth successions of syntactical clauses without emotional repetitions or rhythmic interruptions;[66] and a minimum of parallelism, which helps to bring forth the meaning of the narration.

The most successful and widely known book of Ivanov's first period undoubtedly is *Sady* (1921; second edition, 1922). Like the previous volumes, it is written in a descriptive manner, which much exasperated Gumilëv ("Why does the poet merely see, and not feel; only describe, and not say anything about himself?"[67]) and upset Blok ("'Listening to such terrifying verse about nothing . . . one can begin to cry'").[68]

Sady blossoms in a romantic atmosphere of vagueness, transcience, and uncertain yearnings. At the same time its roots are embedded in classical tradition, which becomes apparent in its happy sense of proportion, remarkable literary taste, simplicity, and restraint. None of the great painters of the Romantic movement had left a lasting impression on Ivanov; but the ethereal charm of Antoine Watteau, as in his "L'embarquement pour Cythère," had captured the poet's imagination. "At some past time," wrote Ivanov, "Watteau touched my heart with his light brush" (*S*, 44).

For Ivanov, beauty did not lie in nature, as such, but in the creative vision of the artist. A sunset is a peacock's fan (*S*, 62); the moon is "a pale disc of a cameo" or seems "woven into the sky by a captive Turkish girl" (*S*, 44, 53); the clouds acquire a yellowish hue "as on a dust-covered engraving" (*S*, 68). Neither nature nor a man's life, but works of art, calling forth aesthetic enjoyment, constituted a positive value. The beauty of a statue, heightened through artistic perception, was superior to life itself:

66. The poem "Petr v Gollandii," dedicated to Anna Axmatova, is a good example.
67. Gumilev, "Pis'ma o russkoj poèzii," *Apollon*, 5:39 (1914).
68. Blok, *Očerki, stat'i i reči* (Moscow, 1955), pp. 300–302.

О, если бы застыть в саду пустынном
Фонтаном, деревом иль изваяньем!

(*S*, 49)

However, next to the sober, impassive artist in Ivanov there also existed a nostalgic dreamer of powerful lyrical persuasion. Throughout his poetic work, now the one and now the other gains the upper hand. In *Sady* the dreamer predominates.

Their vocabulary is highly instrumental in creating their mood of vague, indefinable longings. The most frequent nouns and adjectives are: luna, volny, oblaka, tuman, veter, zakat, muzyka, serdce, zvezdy, ručej, mečta, parusa, lebed' ("lebed' romantizma"), sady, rozy, trevoga, osennij, blednyj, pustoj, sumerečnyj, predzakatnyj, melanxoličnyj, zybkij, dalekij, slabyj, prozračnyj, legkij, tainstvennyj, and tusknejuščij. Often the indefiniteness is further stressed by the suffix -*atyj*: "iz peny rozovatoj" (*S*, 31), "v sinevatom večernem dymu" (*S*, 28), "solonovatyj veter" (*S*, 48); as well as by attenuating adverbs: v otdalen'i, gluxo, vdali, tusklo, and the like. Almost all the verbs have a "waning" quality: they impart the idea of a decrease in action, of negation, or of passivity. Sometimes an infinitive is used to produce this effect: "budet navsegda osuždena vzdyxat'" (*S*, 38,) "ne byt', nazvat' ne mogu" (*S*, 36). The verb "to be" is very often used in the present and is therefore altogether absent, as, for instance, in the first quatrain of the first poem, where only one verb is found, and even that is in the past tense and is joined to "only," which lessens the action:

Где ты, Селим, и где твоя Заира,
Стихи Гафиза, лютня и луна!
Жестокий луч полуденного мира
Оставил сердцу только имена.

(*S*, 7)

In the second quatrain one verb appears in the passive voice (palima), another is negated (ne znaet), and the third has a clearly "decreasing" nature (ronjaet). In another poem, "Ditja garmonii" (*S*, 35), consisting of eight lines, only three verbs appear. Active verbs are usually connected with a question, or else imply a change of status: "esli by stat' voskovoju svečoj" (*S*, 8).

Sady is written in the minor key of the future, signifying a time of unfulfilled dreams and inevitable end, as well as the ever-recurring cycle of life. Evening shadows fall sadly on delicate flowers; their sadness contains an eager longing for the flawlessly beautiful.

An even iambic measure and melodiousness of verse dominate. In Ivanov's later poems these factors play an important role as supporting devices for semantic contrasts. Here and there in *Sady* one comes across a few prosaisms:

> Да, холодно и дров недостает
> И жалкая луна в окно глядится.
>
> (*S*, 46)

The "sapphire robe of sunset" becomes on one occasion "a melon-like horizon" (*S*, 49). Everyday expressions appear, as in the third line of this stanza:

> Я не пойду искать изменчивой судьбы
> В краю, где страусы, и змеи, и лианы.
> Я сел бы в третий класс, и я поехал бы
> Через Финляндию в те северные страны.
>
> (*S*, 66)

The tendency to contrasts is thus gaining deeper significance: a simple opposition of different rhythmic patterns in *Otplyt'e* is giving way to a dramatic contention between form and meaning. Basically, however, *Sady* marks a brief period of harmony, not as a permanent achievement, but only as a point of equilibrium on which two opposing poetical elements have met temporarily in order to proceed in different directions.

THE LATER PERIOD, 1931–1958

> "На грани таянья и льда"
> (Портрет без сходства)

Although Georgij Ivanov had come a long way since his cadet days, when he used to recite verses by Gorodeckij half-seriously and half-jokingly, he remained faithful to the teaching of Nikolaj Gumilëv, who argued that poetry should hypnotize: "in this lies its

strength . . . That is why one should consider as counterfeit verses by
Bunin and other epigones of naturalism—because they are dull,
they do not hypnotize. In their poetry everything is clear and nothing
is beautiful." [69] The poetry of Ivanov fully meets Gumilëv's requirements. It is beautiful mainly because of its elusiveness, its defiance of
exact definition. Its contours are indistinct; its texture mutable. Mist
is the favorite climate in Ivanov's poetical world. People part in fog,
their souls emerge like "fog at dawn" (102), visions of a happy past
glide through the mist. Words denoting a changing condition are
frequent. Half-tones, hints, and unfinished thoughts predominate. It
seems as though the poet were standing on the threshold of emotions
or concepts or of life itself:

> Нет ясной цели. Пустота.
> А там — над Римом — сумрак млечный —
> Ни жизнь ни смерть. Ни свет ни тьма. [70]

"Half" (pòlu-) is the leitmotif of this period: "Polutona rjabiny i
maliny" (58); "Polu-zima, polu vesna" (32). Again:

> Образ полусотворенный,
> Шопот недоговоренный,
> Полужизнь, полуусталость.
> Это все, что мне осталось.
>
>   (27)

The indefiniteness of expressions reinforces the lyrical mood of the
verses and at the same time serves to motivate the poet's stance "on
the border" of things, on the intermediate line that runs between
clearly defined ideas and notions. Xodasevič exemplified this attitude when he likened a poet to a rope walker. [71] By keeping the

69. Gumilev, "Pis'ma o russkoj poèzii," *Apollon*, 10:25 (1910).
70. *Sovremennye zapiski*, 53:210 (1933).
71. Xodasevič, "Akrobat," *Sobranie stixov* (Paris: Vozroždenie, 1927), p. 16.
A parallel occurs in Anatolij Šteiger: "Za celyj den' net tjagostnej minut/ Čem
èta gran': ne son i ne soznan'e." *Sovremennye zapiski*, 67:156 (1938).

> От крыши до крыши протянут канат.
> Легко и спокойно идет акробат.
> В руках его — палка, он весь — как весы...
>
> Поэт, проходи с безучастным лицом:
> Ты сам не таким ли живешь ремеслом?

reader in a state of suspense, the hypnotic value of poetical incantation is greatly heightened. While stable, familiar ideas recede into the background, the relative, fragile ones come to the fore. Ivanov's verse canvas is made of mutation. Its tenuous threads at times come apart, and through the opening, as if from the void, appear weird astral visions:

> Дохнула бездна голубая,
> Меж 'тем' и 'этим' рвется связь.[72]

Everything disintegrates, in order to reappear in another form:

> И тьма — уже не тьма, а свет.
> И да — уже не да, а нет.
> (*О*, 16)

The poet speaks of the rapture of "disincarnation." One critic has called Ivanov "a werewolf, who in the guise of a nightingale sings sweetly—not of young love—but of the wolf's terror on a wintry night."[73] His style, too, is intricate and elusive. It led Adamovič to remark: "What kind of style is this? I asked myself this critical question half-mechanically, from habit or perhaps inertia, preparing to answer it at once, and I had to think about it for a long time. It is not easy to give an answer. The very attempt to formulate it includes the risk of simplifying, smoothing over, flattening out, something that is complex, sickly, continually contradictory and elusive."[74] Ivanov liked to hint at the very essential, then turn it into a joke; begin a phrase, then leave it unfinished:

> Быть может высшая надменность:
> То развлекаться, то скучать,
> Сквозь пальцы видеть современность,
> О самом главном — промолчать.
> (37)

72. *Sovremennye zapiski*, 50:225 (1932).
73. George (Jurij) Ivask, "Georgij Ivanov," *Opyty*, 1:195 (1953).
74. Georgij Adamovič, "Naši poèty; Georgij Ivanov," *Novyj žurnal*, 52:59 (1958).

The elusive quality of Ivanov's verse fulfills a threefold function: it creates the impression of enchantment and lightness, it prepares the ground for the introduction of a foreign element, and it serves as motivation for the poet's "detached" attitude toward his work. One could call the device a "steadfast vacillation," an oxymoron that renders the idea of a constant wavering "on the edge" while maintaining a position of perfect balance.

IMAGERY AND THEMES

An annotation appears in Blok's notebooks under the year 1906: "Every poem is a veil spread out on the spearheads of several words. These words shine like stars. The poem exists because of them." Such key word symbols stand out as landmarks in the work of Georgij Ivanov. At first his symbols represented positive values: hope (ships, sails), beauty (roses, sunsets, stars, music), freedom (the swallow, the swan). Then gradually Ivanov moved in the direction of abstracted metaphor. He took part of an image, one characteristic detail, and ascribed to it an independent existence.[75] The key images began to acquire a different meaning. Sunsets and stars are no longer symbols of beauty and happiness, but act as "breakers" into eternity, into the empty Nothingness. They are still beautiful, yet implacably cruel in their indifference:

> Вымирают города,
> Мужики и господа,
> Старики и детки.
> И глядит на мир звезда
> Сквозь сухие ветки.
>
> (24)

Music, his chief positive element, turns to darkness:

> Пусть себе, как черная стена,
> К звездам подымается она.
> Пусть себе, как черная волна,
> Глухо рассыпается она.
>
> (*O*, 14)

---

75. Compare (30); *O*, 20.

Another frequent image is that of light, expressed by a multitude of nouns, adjectives, and verbs and attenuating elements. A few instances are: "svetozarnoe penie," "v lučax rascveta-uvjadan'ja," "sijaet večnoe stradan'e," "prosijalo v vesennee nebo," "dogorevšej zari niščetu," "blestit zerkal'naja reka," "belizna," "v solnečnoj stolovoj," "v trepete sveta i teni," and "svetlyj sumrak." Almost every line is resplendent with light.[76] What is peculiar, however, is that this emanation has no warmth or joy; quite the contrary, it is closely associated with the cold. Light is not the daily sunshine, warming the earth, but an astral radiance, icy and fair in its purity: "Edva podnjalos' tvoe solnce xolodnoe" (*O*, 58). It is hostile toward men, a double-faced image of life and death. This frigid light is predominantly dark blue:

> Только звезды. Только синий воздух,
> Синий, вечный, ледяной.
>
> (*O*, 18)

Characteristically in Ivanov's poetry, however, the icy ether may suddenly caress, or the cold light shed a tender gleam: "V propasti xoloda nežnogo" (*R*, 22). Next to the icy blue appears a soft rosy hue: "Rozovyj, nežnyj, parižskij zakat" (*R*, 40); "v nebe rozovom do muki" (*R*, 9); "rozoveet zakat—o poslednij byt' možet—vsë nežnej, i nežnej, i nežnej" (*R*, 37). The epithet pink conceals the acute pain felt by the poet for all the beautiful things doomed to fade and disappear in the frigid nimbus of the beyond. In order to reconcile himself with the idea of a cold, engulfing space, Ivanov also peoples it with good-natured, cozy little animals, whom he calls *Razmaxajčiki*.[77]

---

76. See also Adamovič, "Naši poèty," pp. 61–62; Terapiano, "Georgij Ivanov." Ivanov compares Puškin to the "icy irradiance of the star Mair, that has nothing in common with the earth and with which the earth, too, has little in common." "O Pruste," *Čisla*, 1:273 (1930).

77. He introduced them warmly in *Raspad atoma*, pp. 49–53:

"Зверьки были с нами неразлучны... Главными из них были два Размахай-чика... Были и другие зверьки: Голубчик Жухла, Фриштык, Китайчик, глупый Цутик, отвечавший на все вопросы одно и то же — 'Цутик и есть'. Была старая, грубоватая наружно, но нежнейшая в душе Хамка с куцым рыбьим хвостом. Где-то в стороне, непринимаемый в компанию, наводящий неприязнь и страх, водился мрачный фон Клоп.

Ivanov successfully captured the rhythm of his hapless epoch: man's desolateness, his loss of faith in former ideals, his anxiety and skepticism, and despite all, his consuming thirst for happiness. Ivanov's rhythms, as well as his key images, reveal the lyrical ego of the poet, who is jealously guarding the image of Beauty from the deadening triviality of the twentieth century.

In a cycle of poems with the suggestive title *Rayon de Rayonne* (Rayon Shelf), Ivanov portrays coarse *pošlost'*, in such poems as "Na poljanke poutru," "Xudožnikov razvjaznaja maznja," and "Vot bolee il' menee." Yet in the same poems appear such "sunny-lilac" lines as:

> Я твердо решился и тут же забыл
> На что я так твердо решился.
> День влажно-сиренево-солнечный был
> И этим вопрос разрешился.
> Так часто бывает: куда-то спешу
> И в трепете света и тени,
> Сначала раскаюсь, потом согрешу
> И строчка за строчкой навек запишу
> Благоуханье сирени.
>
> (78)

Although often caustic on the topic of émigré life, Ivanov's outlook is mellowed by a sympathetic attitude:

> На южном солнышке болтают старики.
> Они надеются, уже недолго ждать —
> Воскреснет твердый знак, вернутся ять с фитою
> И засияет жизнь эпохой золотою.
>
> (unpub.)

"У зверьков был свой быт, свои привычки, своя философия, своя честь, свои взгляды на жизнь... Они любили танцы, мороженое, прогулки, шелковые банты, праздники, имянины. Они так и смотрели на жизнь. Из чего состоит год? — Из трех сот шестидесяти пяти праздников. — А месяц? — Из тридцати имянин...

"— Зверьки, зверьки, нашептывал им по вечерам из щели страшный фон Клоп, — жизнь уходит, зима приближается. Вас засыпет снегом, вы замерзнете, вы умрете, зверьки — вы, которые так любите жизнь. Но они прижимались тесней друг к другу, затыкали ушки и спокойно, с достоинством, отвечали — 'Это нас не кусается'."

Critics have reproached Ivanov for the restricted range of his themes, which center on Russia, St. Petersburg, émigré life, the conflict between the individual and the machine, and above all, death. Instead of widening his thematic sphere, Ivanov gradually narrowed it, and by so doing, intensified and heightened his message. His poetry achieves a rare fullness and precision of expression and an immediacy of communication. Ivanov had no need for a complete keyboard of themes on which to rely. Like Paganini, he could bewitch his listeners by playing on one string; like a wizard, he could call forth poetry out of nothingness:

> Одни придут другим на смену,
> Но остается колдовство:
> Творить высокое из тлена
> И красоту из ничего![78]

THE DEVICE OF CONTRASTS

> Поэзия: искусственная проза,
> Условное сиянье звездных чар,
> Где улыбаясь произносят — "Роза"
> И с содроганьем думают "Анчар".
>   (79)

Ivanov did not deem it necessary to bridge the gap between incompatibles or to work out a synthesis. Rather, he arrested and made articulate the fleeting manifestations of life. He registered the changing world and the consciousness of his time. "There is no answer to anything. Life poses questions, but does not answer them ... How many beautiful questions have been asked in the course of the world's history, and what answers were given to them!"[79] Man is powerless to harmonize the existing contradictions. In the words of

---

78. Maria Volkova, "Sila slov", *Russkaja mysl'*, October 10, 1959. As Igor' Činnov observed, only the very great poet is able to achieve such an indifference (ravnodušie) to the world and its problems, or perhaps the perception that all problems are indeed of equal importance. As a result, then, for the poet who has reached that "great and very narrow height," any theme, be it universal (death) or intensely personal (one's own eventual death), has equal value, measured only by poetic creation. See his essay "Otvlečenie ot vsego," *Čisla*, 9:206–208 (1933).

79. Ivanov, *Raspad atoma*, p. 61.

another Russian poet, "Now, at the crossroads of all times, it is inopportune even to think of Harmony."[80]

Yet people cannot live without a positive answer. They ask only that someone should disentangle the snarl of confusion and duly shelve each item: Imperial Russia—to the right; present-day Russia —to the left; Russian emigration—to the right, in a special drawer with many subdivisions. Then life becomes simpler. Every person is allotted a suitable place. But where does Ivanov belong? He just does not fit into any of the neatly labeled subdivisions, and worse, he did not even try to fit.

If Ivanov's only concern had been the loss of his homeland, he might have created a myth of absolute values, and thus transformed his own suffering and that of his fellow-countrymen into a consoling emotional catharsis. In that case, he might have been accepted as "their own" and very likely would have lived another ten to twenty years, comforting the souls of the sorrowful exiles with his enchanting verses. But unfortunately for him, Ivanov had the gift of "double sight" ("Mne iskoverkal žizn' talant dvojnogo zren'ja"—55), which prevented him from accepting easy solutions. That is the reason his verse is disquieting. "His poems bite, and people do not like it."[81]

> Я иду по улице, думаю о Боге... О всевозможных гадостях, которые люди делают друг другу. О жалости. О ребенке, просившем у рождественского деда новые глаза для слепой сестры. О том, как умирал Гоголь... Я вспоминаю старую колыбельную: "У кота воркота была мачеха лиха." Я опять возвращаюсь к мысли, что я человек, расположенный быть счастливым... Мы скользим пока по поверхности жизни. По периферии. По синим волнам океана. Видимость гармонии и порядка. Грязь, нежность, грусть. Сейчас мы нырнем. Дайте руку, неизвестный друг.[82]

Only Ivanov's impeccable feeling for measure and artistic balance helped him not to slip from the trivial to the vulgar.

On Ivanov's desk in Paris there still stands a piece of driftwood that he once found on a beach. It resembles a double-faced Janus. When you look at it from one side, the expression is soft and

80. Terapiano, "O čem pisat'?" *Vstreči*, 6 (Paris, 1934).
81. Vladimir Markov, "O poèzii Georgija Ivanova," *Opyty*, 8:87 (1957).
82. Ivanov, *Raspad atoma*, pp. 16–18.

friendly; when you turn it, a grim, almost hostile face confronts you. So, too, are the thematic contrasts that underlie Ivanov's mature lyrics, such as the juxtaposition of pitiless fate and fragile beauty. Beauty, says Ivanov, is merely a fleeting vision; but the hideousness of "world indecency" is long-lived. It will outlast beauty, and in it there can be no meaning, no harmonious synthesis. Beauty is light, a clear blue evening, a "pearly" sky. But at the same time, light can mean evil; in other words, beauty may be a resplendent evil, a "golden slough." The poet mixes white and black: "And darkness is no longer darkness, but light,/and yes is no longer yes, but no" (*O*, 16). There remain neither absolute beauty nor absolute hideousness; even the dividing line between them has vanished. Only the magic of the song remains, created from the "unresolved chaos of sounds," in Annenskij's famous phrase.

Ivanov was able to give new luster and life to ordinary words, to force attention on them by re-evaluating their morphological forms. For example, by pairing the identical forms of the third person plural, past tense, of the verb "padat'" and the genitive singular of the noun "padal'," he makes one more aware of the implications of the word "padali."[83] Or he combines related sounds, like "golubok—klubok," "pod prozračno prizračnoj," "i sliškom ustali i sliškom my stary." Although his lexical arsenal is not spangled with novelty, it unquestionably possesses the element that Henri Bremond called "pure poetry." Petr Bicilli writes about such poetry in general and about Ivanov in particular: "Our times have produced poets—and there are more and more of them—whom it is as pleasant to read as it is difficult to comment on. The direct meaning of their verse is clear at first sight and does not require any elucidation. The poem is not beyond one's understanding; its thought is extremely elementary, —and at the same time it has an unaccountable and irresistible charm ... The most characteristic representative of such poetry seems to me to be Georgij Ivanov."[84]

---

83.   Листья падали, падали, падали
        И никто им не мог помешать...
        От гниющих цветов, как от падали,
        Тяжело становилось дышать.
                    (93)
84. Petr Bicilli, "Vladimir Smolenskij," *Sovremennye zapiski*, 49:450 (1932).

Given the poet's restricted vocabulary, his mastery over words and sounds is achieved by careful selection, arrangement, and semantic antithesis. In his later poems Ivanov fully exploited semantic opposition for poignant effect, as in the lines:

> Вот я иду по осеннему полю,
> Всё как всегда, и другое, чем прежде:
> Точно меня отпустили на волю
> И отказали в последней надежде.
>
> (21)

Often the semantic antithesis is conveyed in words specifically chosen to create a smoothly flowing rhythm. Against this mellow lyric background, the semantic clash acquires new dramatic poignancy:

> Как вы когда-то разборчивы были,
> О, дорогие мои.
> Водки не пили, ее не любили,
> Предпочитали Нюи.
>
> Стал нашим хлебом — цианистый калий,
> Нашей водой — сулема.
> Что ж? Притерпелись и попривыкали,
> Не посходили с ума.
>
> Даже, напротив — в бессмысленно-злобном
> Мире — противимся злу:
> Ласково кружимся в вальсе загробном
> На эмигрантском балу.
>
> (47)

The key word *val's* is supported by even dactyls, while going counter to the semantic design of the poem.

Ivanov sometimes employed the so-called *kol'co stixotvorenija* or "ring-of-verse" structure, with repetition of the opening line or stanza at the end of the poem to close the "ring," for the same purpose of emphasizing the dramatic collision between a beautiful vision and harsh reality. This ring-of-verse structure in Russian lyric poetry is used chiefly in poems where emotion and melody are most important; there is no development in thought, no movement in time, no inner compositional development related to the subject matter. All parts of the poem arise from a common emotional source, and the close, by reiterating the opening line or lines, reverts to the initial mood.[85] Poems such as "Kak v Greciju Bajron" (*R*, 47), "Sijan'e. V dvenadcat' časov" (*O*, 19), "Tol'ko zvezdy" (*O*, 18), and "Svoboden put' pod Fermopilami" (65) illustrate this compositional plan.

Parts of familiar notions or expressions are similarly replaced by their semantic opposites in order to heighten the tragic irony:

> За бессмыслицу! За неудачи!
> За потерю всего дорогого!
> И за то, что могло быть иначе,
> И за то, что не надо другого!
>
> (97)

This device of fraudulent lexical shuffling can be observed in the following poem, which rhythmically parallels Aleksej Pleščeevs' "Lastočka" (The Swallow), known to every Russian child:

> Голубая речка   Травка зеленеет,
> Зябкая волна,   Солнышко блестит,
> Времени утечка   Ласточка с весною
> Явственно слышна.   В сени к нам летит.
>   (73)   (Pleščeev)

The rhyming pattern is similar: abcb in "Lastočka," abab in Ivanov's poem. The syntactical structure of the first two lines is identical: subject and predicate in Pleščeev, attribute and subject in Ivanov. The accentual scheme is also the same, with a stress omission on the second foot, except for the word *golubaja*. By analogy, the Russian reader of Ivanov's poem automatically enters the bright world of childhood. The third line, however, deviates from the previous ones: instead of the joy of welcome, there is a "loss" (utečka), and in the following stanza the grim semantic color darkens, while the playful rhythm remains the same:

> Голубая речка
> Предлагает мне
> Теплое местечко
> На холодном дне.
>
> (73)

85. Cf. Viktor Žirmunskij, *Kompozicija liričeskix stixotvorenij* (Petersburg: Opojaz, 1921), p. 68.

A critic has remarked that these words are "not comforting ones, but the melody is comforting."[86]

In the lexical domain Ivanov seems to exhaust the possible varieties of contrasting parallelisms.[87] The concurrence of opposed images complements his general compositional design. A rose and a trash can are pictured together (62); a dark river bed is opposed to daylight (73); the stars to earth (24), upward movement to a downward fall (77); the lofty to the lowly (41); lightness to heaviness:

> Летний вечер прозрачный и грузный
> Встала радуга коркой арбузной,
> Вьется птица — крылатый булыжник.
>
> (33)

The image of a desert is applied to a metropolis:

> Звезды встают над пустынями
> Ваших волнений и ваших столиц.
>
> (82)

At times Ivanov interweaves several opposing ideas, as in this quotation, where in the space of two lines not only friends and foes,

---

86. Ivask, "Georgij Ivanov," p. 196.
87. Ivanov's last book alone (*Stixi 1943–1958*) furnishes the following examples: "Неизменно...изменилось"; "все как всегда, и другое"; "Что-то сбудется, что-то не сбудется" (21); "Мужики и господа,/Старички и детки" (24); "белые звезды над черным крестом"; "на дне...в вышине"; "Гибнут друзья...торжествуют враги" (28); "вопросы...ответа" (31); "Слова нежны. Сердца пусты" (32); "прозрачный и грузный" (33); "слева...справа" (36); "комары...человечки, умники...дураки" (38); "сегодня ты, а завтра я...кто поутру, кто вечерком"; "белые медведи...рыжие верблюды" (43); "эмблема горя...символ прелести" (47); "идет старик...сидит собака" (48); "Просыпали...подмели" (53); "те...эти" (55); "нелепость...нежность" (56); "распускается...осыпается"(57); "растит...расстреливает"(58); "трезвыми... пьяными" (65); "ученый...неуч" (70); "жизнь потерял, а покой берегу" (75); "осень-весен" (76); "снега и таянья,/Неподвижности и движенья,/ Легкомыслия и отчаянья"; "встают...обрываются" (77); "света...тени" (78); "Богоискатели, бомбометатели" (82); "альпийский холод, нежный зной"; "расцвет...увяданье" (95); "молоды...стары; мертвые...живые; о любви...о разлуке" (97); "мертво внутри...смешно извне" (98); "вспомнить ...забыть"; "погубить...спасти" (102); "встаем-ложимся"; "о прошлом-будущем" (103); "поборники свободы...ревнители ярма"; "хамью... джентельменам" (105); "бессмысленно...неспроста" (107).

but charming foes, disdainful friends, and helpful foes are mingled together:

> Любезные друзья, не стоил я презренья,
> Прелестные враги, помочь вы не могли.
>
> (55)

The oxymoron is a frequent device: "krylatyj bulyžnik" (33), "proxodit tysjača mgnovennyx let" (57), "zatxlyj vozdux svobody ... vol'nyj xolod tjur'my" (60), "pis'ma ot mertvyx druzej polučaju" (75), "Čto svjazyvaet nas? Vsex nas?/Vzaimnoe neponiman'e" (77), and "snačala raskajus', potom sogrešu" (78).

It is with the intention of emphasizing aesthetic values that Ivanov opposes to them the repulsive coarseness of vulgarisms and, in some cases, diminutives, as in:

> Все на свете дело случая —
> Вот нажму на лотерею,
> Денег выиграю кучу я
> И усы, конечно, сбрею.
> Потому что — для чего же
> Богачу нужны усы?
> Много, милостивый Боже,
> В мире покупной красы:
> И нилоны, и часы,
> И вещички подороже.
>
> (90)

Colloquialisms like *nažat' na*, *kuča deneg*, *konečno*, and *dlja čego že* are combined with the Russified *nilon*, the diminutive *veščički*, the poetic *krasa* and the old Slavonic vocative *Bože* to make a caricature of an opportunist. "Zevaja sam ot ètoj temy, ee menjaju na xodu," complains Ivanov, and he recalls Gogol', that great scourger of *pošlost'* and exclaims:

> Как скучно жить на этом свете,
> Как неуютно, господа!
>
> (44)

Ivanov often remembered Gogol' and his words about the trivial, the tragic, and the grotesque in life.

LYRICISM AND THE GROTESQUE

Этой жизни нелепость и нежность.

Дневник

By intermingling dreams with reality, the ridiculous with the fearful, melody with satire, ugliness with beauty, dread with tenderness, and cynical laughter with lyric song, Georgij Ivanov recreated in Russian poetry the genre of lyric grotesque. The devices of contrast and of estranged presentation from "the edge," together with the elements of absurdity and passivity, form the essential ingredients of the grotesque genre. The original meaning of the term, in reference to the paintings in ancient grottoes, carried the idea of heterogeneous detail and bizarre distortion. Thus, the grotesque implies a concatenation of incongruities producing the effect of painful unreality. However, fantastic horror plays only a secondary role; its essential part is an underlying comic element, through which one overcomes the terror. Characteristically, the word "oxymoron," often associated with this genre, is a compound of these two notions: *oxys*—sharp, and *mōros*—foolish.

Just as the surmounting of the horror element, manifested in the grotesque distortion of forms, produces laughter, so the overcoming of the grotesque in Ivanov's poetry leads to a still stronger lyric emotion. The grotesque may be said to be based upon two dimensions: the laughable-horizontal and the frightening-vertical. The lyric veil of Ivanov's poetry is likewise spread out over an abyss: as you move along the surface, you feel the pull of the chasm.

Some wonder why Ivanov considered it necessary to add drops of poison to his melodious balm.[88] "A ot cevo? Nikto ne vedaet pritcyny," the poet maliciously retorts, and goes on mixing his potion of the absurd, the lyric, the laughable, and the tragic.

А от цево? Никто не ведает притцыны...

Fonvizin, *Korion*, Act I, scene 2

По улице уносит стружки
Ноябрьский ветер ледяной.
— Вы русский? — Ну, понятно, *рушкий*.
Нос бесконечный. Шарф смешной.

---

88. "Osvobodjas' ot šeluxi/Nenužnyx slov . . ./Napišem novye stixi/O vetre v pole i o Boge." Jurij Trubeckoj, "Georgiju Ivanovu," *Vozroždenie*, 18:110 (1951).

Есть у него жена и дети,
Своя мечта, своя беда...
Как скучно жить на этом свете,
Как неуютно, господа!

Обедать, спать болеть поносом.
Немножко красть. — А кто не крал?
...Такой же Гоголь с длинным носом
Так долго, страшно умирал...

(44)

In this poem appear the main features of the grotesque: the odd distortions of form, of phonetics and spelling (*cevo, ruškij*), of syntax (*takoj že Gogol'*), and of substance (the portrait of the passerby). Amid this ridicule appears the long-nosed face of the dying writer.

The device of estrangement grows in significance. Ivanov had always stood at an intermediate point between contrasting positions; he now stands farther and farther away from everything, viewing it all as strange. The universe ceases to be a cozy, sheltered place into which no astral winds can penetrate. The doors stand ajar and may be thrown open at any moment, admitting the terrifying incertitude of the void. The transition from the here to the beyond and vice versa becomes easy; everything grows lighter, colder, more and more disquieting: "Pis'ma ot mertvyx druzej polučaju" (75), "Laskovo kružimsja v val'se zagrobnom" (47), "Možet i sovsem ne ptička, a iz ada golosok?" (45). *Razmaxajčiki*, those astral little animals with long thin tails, make themselves at home in the rooms. They too recall grotesque paintings, where the animal and human worlds have no marked boundaries. While people experience "something cat-like or bird-like" (105), the animal world acquires human characteristics, as in paintings by Hieronymus Bosch ("The Devil") or Daumier ("The Unexpected"). This last picture represents a horse's head and two front hoofs standing in a doorway, to the horror of the master of the house, who has just opened the door to this "guest."

The realm of the fantastic is a common source of inspiration to both the lyric and the grotesque genres. A lyric poem expresses the poet's subjective experience, while the device of the grotesque is his means of distorting objective reality: both are subjective and fantastic. In Ivanov's work, inanimate things talk and animate beings seem soulless automatons:[89]

> Встают — встаю. Садятся — сяду.
> Стозначный помню номер свой.
>
> (67)

The sense of reality and proportion seems lost in a whirlpool of inconsistencies and fancy, just as in Gogol''s words: "Už ne son li vse èto—Rossija, Peterburg, snega, podlecy, departamenty, kafedra, teatry." Ivanov's "unforgettable Petersburg" is also a phantom, disappearing in "dim fog." No sounds disturb the specter-world. In the distance a pale reflection, a mere shadow, noiselessly walks along the paths of the Summer Garden: "Po pustynnym allejam neslyšno projdu" (99). The world is no longer a cosmos. Its relativity is laid bare. Nothing is stable: people, objects, and concepts sway, change, move, and vanish.

> Не станет ни России, ни Америки,
> Ни Царскосельских парков, ни Москвы —
> Припадок атомической истерики
> Все распылит в сияньи синевы.
>
> (92)

The element of pity is excluded from the grotesque. What excites mirth cannot be tragic in the full sense of the word and does not evoke compassion. People are not people but puppets—"mertvo vnutri—smešno izvne"—or caricatures.

The device of absurdity destroys logical and causal connections, just as the mask severs the link between outer form and its content, between appearance and substance, which leads to a cleavage in personality. This theme is developed by Ivanov in his book *Raspad atoma*. In this cleft between the tender and the bizarre Ivanov's poetry has its roots. At times one wonders whether the mask is laughing at the man or the man is playing with the mask. Where does the poet stand: on the side of the tormented émigré, who wished

89. Compare Roman Jakobson's discussion of similar devices used by Xlebnikov and Majakovskij, in his *Novejšaja russkaja poèzija* (Prague, 1921), pp. 14–16.

nothing better than plain human happiness; or on the side of the pitiless-merciful Fate, which sweeps away all suffering into the "azure brightness"? The riddle remains. "V moix slovax žestokaja zagadka." The mask and the face now merge, now split. Art is a diverting play; Ivanov an excellent player. At one point he sketched what may be a self-portrait:

> Я бы зажил, зажил заново
> Не Георгием Ивановым,
> А слегка очеловеченным,
> Энергичным, щеткой вымытым,
> Вовсе роком не отмеченным,
> Первым встречным-поперечным,
> Всё равно какое имя там...
>
> (70)
>
> Я хотел бы улыбнуться,
> Отдохнуть, домой вернуться...
> Я хотел бы так немного,
> То, что есть почти у всех,
> Но что мне просить у Бога
> И бессмыслица и грех.
>
> (66)

He labeled it: A Portrait Without Resemblance (Portret bez sxodstva). It is useless to question, "Where, then, *is* the real Ivanov?" He is in each one of his poems—in the leering grin of the mask as well as the tender smile. He will speak about various things in an enticing fashion, but as soon as one asks him about "the most important thing," he will fall silent, smile, and slip away. Although the necessary historical perspective to draw a complete picture of Ivanov's place in Russian poetry is still lacking, the data gathered here may nevertheless help to make it "a portrait with resemblance."

At the present time Ivanov's name still incites heated argument, in which personal feelings are not totally absent. Among those who recognize his poetical merits, this opinion is characteristic: "In Georgij Ivanov is concentrated the whole quintessence of both positive and negative literary and aesthetic emotions of the early years of emigration. Notwithstanding an ethical 'cleavage' and the extreme refinement of some of his lines, only in him is still powerful the tradition of a great creative legacy and of an inexhaustible lyricism.

In his work he transcends the emigration period and enters the pantheon of Russian poetry."[90]

The sad and at the same time important destiny of Georgij Ivanov was to become the only real poet of Russian emigration with the manifold complexities and sorrows of that life. His work could only have been written by a man who had grown up in Russia, but whose whole period of literary maturation and maturity belonged to the years in exile. His poetry is hybrid in character: it is the expression of the spirit of an internal émigré in the context of a fully assimilated native Russian tradition. It is thoroughly unlike the work of the older Russian poets cast out to the West by the Revolution. The émigré years of an artist such as Xodasevič, for example, are only a poetic epilogue to a rich and productive life in a fully Russian environment. Ivanov's poetry differs as well from the work of the gifted younger Russian poets in Western Europe and America. Russia's culture came to them more as a kind of reminiscence, so that their poetry was devoid of the fundamental duality that characterizes both the life and the poetic work of Georgij Ivanov.

90. Nikolaj Berner, "Razgovor s muzami," *Literaturnyj sovremennik*, Munich, 1954, p. 260.

Bibliography

WORKS BY GEORGIJ VLADIMIROVIČ IVANOV

Verse

Many individual poems, often with minor variant readings, appeared in journals and newspapers, although they usually were later included in one or more of the books. They are itemized in the Harvard dissertation by Ludmila A. Foster, *Bibliography of Russian Émigré Literature, 1918–1968*, 1969.

Otplyt'e na ostrov Citeru. Stixi. St. Petersburg: Ego, 1912.

Gornica. Kniga stixov. St. Petersburg: Giperborej, 1914. 63 pp., 52 poems, many reprinted from *Otplyt'e*.

Pamjatnik slavy. Stixotvorenija. Petrograd: Lukomor'e, 1915. 79 pp., 31 poems.

Veresk. Vtoraja kniga stixov. Moscow-Petrograd: Al'ciona, 1916. 109 pp., 28 new poems, 27 taken from *Otplyt'e* and *Gornica*. Second edition, Berlin: Z. I. Gržebin, 1923. 85 pp., 46 poems (three new), seven translations from French poets.

Sady. Tret'ja kniga stixov. Petrograd: Petropolis, 1921. 91 pp., 43 poems. Second edition, Berlin: Z. I. Gržebin, 1922.

Lampada. Sobranie stixotvorenija, Kniga pervaja. Petrograd: Mysl', 1922. 123 pp., 40 new poems, 46 from earlier volumes. Second edition, Petrograd: Mysl', 1923.

Rozy. Paris: Rodnik, 1931. 60 pp., 41 poems.

Otplytie na ostrov Citeru. Izbrannye stixi 1916–1936. Berlin: Petropolis, 1937. 103 pp.; 20 new poems, 37 from *Rozy*, 21 from *Veresk* and *Sady*.

Portret bez sxodstva. Stixi. Paris: Rifma, 1950. 43 pp., 39 poems headed "Portret bez sxodstva" and 10 labeled "Rayon de Rayonne."

Stixi 1943–1958. New York: Novyj žurnal, 1958. With an introduction by Roman Gul' (pp. 5–16). 112 pp. This volume is made up of "Portret bez sxodstva" (omitting seven poems that were in the 1958 edition and adding three new ones), "Rayon de Rayonne" (with five new poems), and "Dnevnik," a new collection of 79 poems.

Prose

Peterburgskie zimy. Paris: Rodnik, 1928. 189 pp. Second edition, New York: Chekhov, 1952. With an introduction by Vjačeslav Zavorišin (pp. 7–15). 240 pp.

Raspad atoma. Paris: Dom knigi, 1938. 87 pp.
"Žizel'," *Illjustrirovannaja Rossija*, No. 191, Paris, 1929.
"Četvertoe izmerenie," *Illjustrirovannaja Rossija*, No. 214, Paris, 1929.
"Dama s Bel'vedera," *Illjustrirovannaja Rossija*, No. 222, Paris, 1929.
"Vasilisa," *Illjustrirovannaja Rossija*, No. 225, Paris 1929.
Tretij Rim (unfinished novel). Part I in *Sovremennye zapiski*, 39:75–124 (1929), 40:211–237 (1929); Part II in *Čisla* 3:26–54 (1930).
"General'ša Lizan'ka," *Illjustrirovannaja Rossija*, No. 346, Paris, 1931.
Nasten'ka, a short novel. From a family chronicle (unfinished). *Vozroždenie*, 12 (1950).

The advertisements in the back of *Veresk* (1916) list two books of fiction "in press" (*Venera s priznakami*—a short novel, and *Pervaja kniga rasskazov*) and two scholarly works "in preparation" (*Russkie vtorostepennye poèty XVIII veka*—studies and anthology, and *Aleksandr Poležaev* —critical study). No further information about these four works has come to light.

Translations

Coleridge, Samuel Taylor. *Christabel.* Berlin: Petropolis, 1923.
Voltaire, François-Marie Arouet. *La Pucelle d'Orléans* (*Orleanskaja devstvennica*), 2 vols. In collaboration with Georgij Adamovič and Nikolaj Gumilev. Petrograd: Vsemirnaja literatura, 1924.
Perse, Saint-John. *Anabase* (*Anabazis*). In collaboration with Georgij Adamovič. Paris: Ja. E. Povolockij: 1926.

Articles and Reviews

"Stixi v žurnalax 1912 g.," *Apollon*, 1:75 (1913).
"Voennye stixi," *Apollon*, 1:58 (1915).
"O novyx stixax," *Apollon*, 3:51 (1915).
"Voennye stixi," *Apollon*, 4–5:82 (1915).
"Stixi o Rossii Aleksandra Bloka," *Apollon*, 8–9:96 (1915).
"Stixi v žurnalax, izdatel'stva, al'manaxi, kružki v 1915 g.," *Apollon*, 1:59 (1916).
"O novyx stixax," *Apollon*, 6–7:71 (1916).
"Počtovyj jaščik," *Cex poètov*, 4:65 (Berlin, 1923).
"Kitajskie teni," *Zveno*, 158:9, 164:5, 195:9 (1926), 205:8–11, 210:6–8, 218:5–7 (1927).
"Kannegiser," in *Leonid Kannegiser, 1918–1928*, Stat'i G. Adamoviča, M. A. Aldanova, G. Ivanova (Paris: L. Beresniak, 1928), pp. 39–52.
"Anketa o Pruste," *Čisla*, 1:272 (1930).
"V. Sirin. Mašen'ka; Korol', dama, valet; Zaščita Lužina; Vozvraščenie Čorba," *Čisla*, 1:233 (1930).
"Xolčev, A. 'Gong'; 'Smertnyj plen,'" *Čisla*, 2–3:267 (1930).
"K jubileju V. F. Xodeseviča, Privet čitatelja," *Čisla*, 2–3:311 (1930). Signed A. Kondrat'ev.

156 *Irina Agushi*

"Buket ljubitelja prekrasnogo na grud' zarubežnoj slovesnosti," *Čisla*, 2–3:31:314 (1930). Signed Ljubitel' prekrasnogo.
"O Gumileve," *Sovremennye zapiski*, 47:306 (1931).
"Bez čitatelja," *Čisla*, 5:148 (1931).
"Boris Poplavskij. Flagi. Izd. *Čisla*, Pariž, 1931," *Čisla*, 5:231 (1931).
"O novyx russkix ljudjax," *Čisla*, 7–8:184 (1933).
"Pamjati Vjačeslava Ivanova," *Vozroždenie*, 5:162 (1949).
"Blok i Gumilev," *Vozroždenie*, 6:113 (1949).
'Pamjati knjagini S. A. Volkonskoj," *Vozroždenie*, 7:178 (1950).
"Literatura i žizn'," *Vozroždenie*, 8:192 (1950).
"Tri poèta," *Vozroždenie*, 9:198 (1950).
"Literatura i žizn'," *Vozroždenie*, 10:179 (1950).
"Istoki Aldanova," *Vozroždenie*, 10:182 (1950).
"Literatura i žizn'. Konec Adamoviča," *Vozroždenie*, 11:179 (1950).
"Novosel'e na novosel'e," *Vozroždenie*, 11:187 (1950).
"Zakat nad Peterburgom," *Vozroždenie*, 27:178 (1953).
"Roman Gul'. Kon' ryžij," *Novyj žurnal*, 34:304 (1953).
"Osip Mandel'štam," *Novyj žurnal*, 43:273 (1955).
"Georgij Adamovič. Odinočestvo i svoboda," *Novyj žurnal*, 43:296 (1955).
"A. M. Remizovu," *Opyty*, 8:127 (1957).

Volumes Edited and Introduced

Gumilev, Nikolaj. *Stixotvorenija*, Posmertnyj sbornik. 2nd ed. Petrograd: Mysl', 1923.
———. Pis'ma o russkoj poèzii. Petrograd: Mysl', 1923.
———. Čužoe nebo. 2nd ed. Berlin: Petropolis, 1936.
Esenin, Sergej. Izbrannye stixi. Paris: Vozroždenie, 1951.

WORKS ON GEORGIJ IVANOV

Adamovič, Georgij. "Naši poèty. 1. Georgij Ivanov," *Novyj žurnal*, 52:55 (1958).
———. "Literaturnye besedy," *Zveno*, 174:2 (1926).
Aldanov, Mark (pseud. for Mark Landau). "Georgij Ivanov. *Peterburgskie zimy*," *Sovremennye zapiski*, 37:526–526–528 (1928).
Bicilli, Petr. "Georgij Ivanov. 'Otplytie na ostrov Citeru. Izbrannye stixi 1916–1936,'" *Sovremennye zapiski*, 64:458 (1937).
Bik, È. P. "Literaturnye kraja," *Krasnaja nov'*, 2:351 (1922).
Bol'šuxin, Jurij. "Arterial'noe davlenie," *Novoe russkoe slovo*, September 6, 1959.
Červinskaja, Lidija. "Posle panixidy," *Russkaja mysl'*, September 27, 1958.
G. "Georgij Ivanov. Peterburgskie zimy," *Opyty*, 1:193 (1953).
Gippius, Zinaida. "Čerty ljubvi. Doklad v obščestve 'Zelenaja lampa.'" *Krug*, Al'manax, 3:139 (1938).
Gul', Roman. "Georgij Ivanov," *Novyj žurnal*, 42:110 (1955).

Gumilev, Nikolaj. "Pis'mo o russkoj poèzii," *Apollon*, 5:34 (1914).
——. "Pis'mo o russkoj poèzii," *Apollon*, 1:27 (1916).
Ivask, George (Jurij). "Portret bez sxodstva G. Ivanova," *Opyty*, 1:195 (1953).
——. "Pamjati Georgija Ivanova," *Opyty*, 9:4 (1958).
Jakonovskij, Evgenij. "Georgij Ivanov v opale," *Russkaja mysl'*, September 13, 1958.
K. F. "Poslednij svidetel' 'Serebrjanogo veka,'" *Posev*, September 7, 1958.
Markov, Vladimir. "O poèzii Georgija Ivanova," *Opyty*, 8:83 (1957).
——. "Georgij Ivanov. 1943–1958. Stixi," *The Slavic and East European Journal*, 17:286 (1959).
——. "Russkie citatnye poèty: zametki o poèzii P. A. Vjazemskogo i Georgija Ivanova," *To Honor Roman Jakobson*, II, 1273–1287 (The Hague, 1967).
Ocup, Nikolaj. "Pamjati Georgija Ivanova," *Russkaja mysl'*, September 9, 1958.
Ofrosimov, Jurij. "Georgij Ivanov. Sady, 1921," *Novaja russkaja kniga*, 2:21 (1922).
——. "Georgij Ivanov. Lampada, Petrograd, 1922," *Novaja russkaja knija*, 7:11 (1922).
Oksenov, Innokentij. "Georgij Ivanov. Sady. Peterburg, 1921," *Kniga i revoljucija*, 3:72 (1922).
——. "Georgij Ivanov. Lampada. Mysl', Petrograd, 1922," *Kniga i revoljucija*, 7:62 (1922).
Perfil'ev, Aleksandr. "Georgij Ivanov," *Novoe russkoe slovo*, September 21, 1958.
Poljanin, Andrej. "Georgij Ivanov. Sady. 3-ja kniga stixov. Petropolis 1921," *Šipovnik*, 1:177 (1922).
Pomerancev, Kirill. "Poèzija Georgija Ivanova," *Russkaja mysl'*, August 12, 1958.
Potëmkin, P. P. "Georgij Ivanov. Sady. Tret'ja kniga stixov. Izd. Petropolis, 1921, Peterburg," *Novosti literatury*, 1:55 (1922).
Prošin, Kasjan (pseud. for Anatolij Beklemišev). "O tvorčestve Georgija Ivanova," *Novoe russkoe slovo*, November 30, 1958.
Šik, Aleksandr. "Pamjati Georgija Ivanova," *Russkaja mysl'*, September 18, 1958.
Sirin, Vladimir (pseud. for Vladimir Nabokov). Review of "Literaturnyj smotr," *Sovremennye zapiski*, 70:283 (1940).
Smolenskij, Vladimir. "Portret bez sxodstva G. Ivanova," *Vozroždenie*, 32:141 (1954).
Struve, Gleb. *Russkaja literatura v izgnanii*, pp. 315–318, 320–324 (New York: Chekhov, 1956).
Tatiščev, Nikolaj. "Stixi Georgija Ivanova," *Russkaja mysl'*, November 27, 1958.

Terapiano, George (Jurij). "O poèzii Georgija Ivanova," *Literaturnyj sovremennik* (Munich), 1954, p. 240.

———. "Georgij Ivanov, 1943–1958. Stixi," *Russkaja mysl'*, November 8, 1958.

———. "Pamjati Georgija Ivanova," *Russkaja mysl'*, August 31, 1958.

Vejdle, Vladimir. "O 'Rozax,'" *Vozroždenie* (newspaper), May 28, 1937.

Xodasevič, Vladislav. "Knigi i ljudi. Otplytie na ostrov Citeru," *Vozroždenie* (newspaper), May 28, 1937.

Zavališin, Vjačeslav. Introduction to *Peterburgskie zimy*, pp. 7–15. New York: Chekhov, 1952.

Zlobin, Vladimir. "Čelovek i naši dni," in *Literaturnyj smotr*, p. 158. Paris, 1939.

POEMS DEDICATED TO GEORGIJ IVANOV

Berberova, Nina. "Nevermore," in Ivask, Jurij, ed. *Na zapade*, p. 101. New York: Chekhov, 1953.

Mamčenko, Viktor. "Georgiju Ivanovu," *Sovremennye zapiski*, 56:202 (1934).

Mandel'štam, Osip. "Carskoe selo," in *Kamen'*, p. 50. New York: Chekhov, 1955.

Pomerancev, Kirill. "Georgiju Ivanovu," *Opyty*, 2:20 (1953).

———. "Na smert' Georgija Ivanova," *Russkaja mysl'*, October 14, 1958.

Prismanova, Anna. "Georgiju Ivanovu," *Sovremennye zapiski*, 70:126 (1940).

Trubeckoj, Jurij. "Georgiju Ivanovu," *Vozroždenie*, 18:110 (1951).

———. "Pamjati Georgija Ivanova," *Russkaja mysl'*, January 29, 1959.

Volkova, Maria. "Sila slov," *Russkaja mysl'*, October 10, 1959.